UNSTOPPABLE!

UNSTOPPABLE!

MY JOURNEY FROM WORLD CHAMPION TO ATHLETE A TO 8-TIME NCAA NATIONAL GYMNASTICS CHAMPION AND BEYOND

MAGGIE NICHOLS

WITH HOPE INNELLI

Roaring Brook Press
New York

Please take note that this book contains content
that may be sensitive to some readers, including:
sexual abuse and eating disorders.

Published by Roaring Brook Press
Roaring Brook Press is a division of Holtzbrinck
Publishing Holdings Limited Partnership
120 Broadway, New York, NY 10271 • fiercereads.com

Our books may be purchased in bulk for promotional, educational,
or business use. Please contact your local bookseller or the Macmillan
Corporate and Premium Sales Department at (800) 221-7945 ext.
5442 or by email at MacmillanSpecialMarkets@macmillan.com.

Library of Congress Cataloging-in-Publication Data
Names: Nichols, Maggie, 1997– author.
Title: Unstoppable! : my journey from Olympic hopeful to Athlete A to
  eight-time NCAA champion and beyond / Maggie Nichols ; with Hope Innelli.
Description: First edition. | New York : Roaring Brook Press, 2024. | Audience:
  Ages 14–18 | Audience: Grades 10–12 | Summary: "Maggie Nichols' official
  memoir is an inspirational tell-all about the abuse she suffered under the USA
  national gymnastic team and how she managed to redefine herself in the face of
  adversity. *Content warning for: sexual abuse"—Provided by publisher.
Identifiers: LCCN 2023024466 | ISBN 9781250860224 (hardcover) |
  ISBN 9781250860231 (ebook)
Subjects: LCSH: Nichols, Maggie, 1997—Juvenile literature. | USA Gymnastics—
  Juvenile literature. | University of Oklahoma—Gymnastics—Juvenile literature. |
  Sexual abuse victims—United States—Biography—Juvenile literature. |
  Women gymnasts—United States—Biography—Juvenile literature.
Classification: LCC GV460.2.N53 A3 2024 | DDC 796.44092 [B]—dc23/
  eng/20230817
LC record available at https://lccn.loc.gov/2023024466

First edition, 2024
Book design by Abby Granata
Printed in the United States of America by Lakeside
Book Company, Harrisonburg, Virginia

ISBN 978-1-250-86022-4
1 3 5 7 9 10 8 6 4 2

To my parents, coaches, and mentors throughout the years,
with love and gratitude.

TABLE OF CONTENTS

UNSTOPPABLE!

INTRODUCTION
FROM SIMONE BILES

C ome hang out with us." Those were probably the first words I said to Maggie. We were about fourteen years old and attending one of the national training camps for gymnastics in Houston, Texas. We spent a week there once a month, staying in cabins on a ranch. I had already been to a few of them, but it was Maggie's first one. The camps can be nerve-racking, because all the gymnasts want to show their best work and want to be invited back to continue training to be on the national team and compete at the World Championships, international competitions, and hopefully the Olympics. I knew how stressful the camps could be, and remembered that at my first one some of the older girls embraced us, took us under their wing, and showed us the ropes. I wanted to do that for Maggie. She and her roommate were a few doors down from me, and I remember going into her room after practice when a bunch of us were hanging out. Maggie was kind of quiet, and I said, "Come hang out with us." She said, "No, I'm okay. I going to get some rest." I insisted, begging, and told her it wasn't going to work for her to be alone in the room. I don't know why, but I could feel her energy and felt like she was going to be a good friend. So I pulled her away from her shell and made her hang out with us.

Ever since then, we have been best friends. Maggie was very shy in the beginning. And my personality is big and loud (especially when I was youn-ger). I'm always cheering people up and making them laugh, and I think I brought that side out of Maggie. Whenever we were together, we were always laughing. I don't even remember about what—usually it was over small and silly things. We immediately bonded, because even though our personalities are different, we shared so many other things. We both have dogs and shared our romantic crushes. We talked about everything but gymnastics, from school to boys and other dumb stuff that builds a forever friendship. Getting ready for practice, we were always having a good time, dancing and laughing. We were a good balance for each other. Maggie was so levelheaded in the gym, and she taught me that once we're in the gym, it's business first and fun later. And I taught her that once business is over, we could have fun, be goofy, and be fifteen- and sixteen-year-olds. And that at the end of the day, gymnastics is what we do, and not who we are—it's just a part of our lives.

The national gymnastics staff knew Maggie and I were good friends, so if we were assigned to the same competition, we got to room together. We have been through so much together, including winning a World Championships victory as a team. Some people have asked how we can be friends when we were competing against each other, but we never saw it that way. Maggie always said, "I want to vault like you," so when she trained vault, I would encourage and help her. She's good at bars and beam and one of the most consistent gymnasts I've ever met, and I tried to emulate that. We weren't competitive and were never jealous of the other; we learned from each other and supported and guided each other.

When Maggie decided to go to University of Oklahoma (OU) and compete at the collegiate level, her success didn't surprise me, because she was already an amazing gymnast at the elite level, and she got even better, which is crazy because she kept it up for four years. I visited her there and stayed with her. We hadn't seen each other in a couple of years, but it was just like old times when we were competing together. We got ice cream and had so much fun. I loved supporting and watching her. She has one of the best collegiate careers I've ever seen, and I'm not just saying that because I'm biased as her best friend. She was so poised, consistent, and one of the most beautiful gymnasts to watch. She's quiet, but a leader. Once she steps into that role, she takes it on fully. She turned things around for gymnastics at OU and will forever be one of their sports legends for what she accomplished there.

We're adults now and we are both so busy, but we still text to stay in touch. And, when we talk, we always just pick up like no time has passed. That's what is so special about our friendship—we don't have to talk every day to know we still support each other. She came to my wedding and supported me, and she's engaged now, so I'm excited about that. I hope to be there to support her on her big day too—just like we were there for each other on big days in our gymnastics careers. Our accomplishments are different now that we're older—she graduated from college, I got married and went back to training, and she got engaged and is working now—but we're just as excited for each other as we were when we won Worlds.

When I was recently deciding whether to return to training after taking some time off, Maggie and I talked about it. And of course she said it was crazy but she supported me 100 percent. She said, "If anybody can do it, it's you." I love her for that. We talked about the surgeries she's had, and how she's trying to get her knees healthy and start a new chapter in her life as a fitness trainer. Maggie is one of the strongest people I know, and she always showed up for me. I'm going to do the same. That's what I value so much about our friendship. It's nice to have a friend like that.

— *Simone*

PREFACE

Have you ever loved something so much you were willing to sacrifice almost anything for it? Sleep? Food? A social life?

That's how I felt about gymnastics. As far back as I can remember, it was something that made me really happy. You've seen the T-shirts, gym bags, and leotards emblazoned with the words TODAY'S GOOD MOOD IS SPONSORED BY GYMNASTICS! Well, that's how gymnastics made me feel all the time when I was a kid. But I didn't just love the sport; I wanted to be the very best in it.

I worked hard to climb the ranks quickly. As a young child, I trained at Twin City Twisters, one of the best gyms in the country. By age fourteen, I began training once a month at the USA Gymnastics camp at the Karolyi Ranch in Huntsville, Texas. That's where, for a long time, Olympians were made.

By 2013, I was a proud member of the US national team. I competed in overseas events, representing the United States throughout the world. But behind the scenes, my story started to take more twists and turns than a triple double.

My elite gymnastics career was marked by some extreme highs and lows. The most notable high was my role in helping the US team win the gold medal at the 2015 World Championships, and among the most notable lows was not being named to the 2016 Olympic Team just a few months later, despite being favored to be one of the five members, or an alternate. After the breakout year I'd had leading up to the Olympics, I was shocked by the decision, as were many others involved in the sport.

* * *

It is widely believed that I was snubbed because I was the first athlete on the national team to report Larry Nassar's sexual abuse to USA Gymnastics. I was also the first to ask in concern if he had abused others. And later, I was the first of the team members to join the civil suit against Nassar and those who had failed to supervise him and protect the young people in his midst: Michigan State University (MSU), USA Gymnastics, and the US Olympic & Paralympic Committee.

In my view of the situation, USA Gymnastics had strong reasons to want to keep the revelations quiet. The news threatened to damage its reputation and the sport, and possibly disrupt the upcoming Olympics, not to mention the bid to host the 2024 or 2028 Olympics. It was explosive. In time, Nassar's crimes would become the biggest sexual abuse scandal in all of sports history.

With my Olympic dreams dashed, I headed to University of Oklahoma (OU) to compete for their gymnastics team, the Sooners, and I'm proud to say that I ended up on top. I became an eight-time NCAA champion, winning two team championships and six individual champion titles, thereby solidifying my standing as one of the best all-time gymnasts at the collegiate level.

As awesome as my college years were, there were still some challenges I had to face. In the early court filings against Larry Nassar, I was listed as Athlete A for my own protection. It was during my sophomore year that I made the choice, despite being an intensely private person, to identify myself publicly so others who had been wronged by Nassar could feel comfortable coming forward too. I didn't want anyone affected by him to feel unseen or unheard.

I also wrote an impact statement to be read at Nassar's conviction and sentencing. Thankfully, then Detective Sergeant Andrea Munford and then Assistant Attorney General for the state of Michigan, Angela Povilaitis, fought for all of the survivors' First Amendment rights to do so because it was important that Nassar's crimes not just be reduced to a number—as staggering as that number was. They felt it was important that Nassar and the world see and hear from those of us whose lives he had so drastically affected.

In 2020, during my senior year at OU, my final competitive gymnastics season was abruptly cut short by the Covid-19 pandemic. Many of your own hopes and plans were put on hold or prematurely ended during that time too, so I know you can understand how let down I felt when fate denied me one last chance to leave everything I had on the competition floor in the sport I love so much.

Fortunately, when in-person classes resumed, I was able to continue as a student assistant coach for the Sooners while I worked my way through my master's degree in intercollegiate administration.

I also continued the long fight for justice, appearing before the US Senate Judiciary Committee to make sure that others who enabled Nassar or who were negligent in the handling of the investigation were held accountable as well. These efforts are still ongoing.

I've shared a lot about my life with you already, but if you think this rundown of events is the whole story, you would be wrong. *These are just the headlines.*

Although I prefer keeping to myself most of the time, I'm writing about all my experiences in and out of the gym, including many details never shared before, because I think it is important for people to understand that no single success or disappointment in life defines who we are. I know it's been said before, but we really are the sum of *all* our experiences. Who I am as a person influenced my gymnastics career as much as who I am as an athlete. It is wonderful to celebrate our victories, but the celebration is half-hearted if we don't also appreciate the sacrifices, the challenges, the disappointments, the course corrections, and the growth that comes from how we handled the circumstances that were beyond our control. I think it is in these details that champions are made.

Throughout this book I share the guiding principles and values that helped me on my journey. I hope the reflections in these pages inspire you to be the best you can be and that they help you cope in the times when you are struggling. But most of all, I hope they convince you that you are always stronger than you think.

♡ *Maggie*

CHAPTER ONE
DRIVE

It's not how bad you want it; it's about
how hard you're willing to work for it.

—ANONYMOUS

I know you're not supposed to wish for things; you're supposed to work for them. But when I was a child, I used to ask my parents for spare change every time we went to the Maplewood Mall near our home in Little Canada, Minnesota. I would toss the coins in the fountain, and my wish was always the same. My one true desire was to compete in the Olympics someday. I wanted to represent the United States as an elite-level gymnast.

I remember watching Carly Patterson, the all-around champion, on TV during the 2004 Summer Olympics in Athens, Greece. I rushed outside during commercial breaks to "try" all the flips she was flawlessly executing. We had this big square patch of grass with slightly curved corners in our front yard that always looked to me like a floor exercise. I ran toward it as fast as I could and did some of my best skills at the time. I began with a round-off back handspring back tuck, imagining that I was doing what Carly did on her first pass. Then I improvised some more, doing a front handspring front tuck as if it was just like her other pass. I followed that by a few leaps and some dancing. When the competition resumed on television, my mom called me back inside. I was only six years old, but I knew then that I wanted to do exactly what Carly was doing someday.

It was a big dream for sure, but it wasn't an unrealistic one. I really believe that I was born to do gymnastics. When I was a baby, my parents couldn't keep me in my crib. I would climb out of it every night and end up in their bedroom. The next morning, they would wonder, *How did she get in here? She can't even walk!* By the time I was a toddler, I was tumbling on the couch cushions and leaping over the backyard fence. I can't explain it. It's just what I did.

When I was three years old, my parents decided to put me in a local gymnastics class in Roseville, Minnesota. They thought I'd be safer if I learned some basic techniques. They brought my brother Danny along as well, but he didn't last too long. He was too much of a playful distraction for me, and the coaches suspected by then that if I gave gymnastics my focus, great things could come of it.

My parents, and my older brothers, Steve, Sam, and Danny, are all athletic. The boys played baseball, basketball, football, and lacrosse. My dad played every sport imaginable in his youth, and my mom was into high school gymnastics. They're still very active today, so I suppose it was just in my genes.

I guess you could say I was naughty in the gym. I definitely listened to the coaches. I did whatever they asked me to do and made every correction I was given, but I would skip the line all the time so I could take more turns than the other girls. All that extra practice was how I got good at doing back handsprings before everyone else my age. When the coaches saw me always angling to have another try, they could just tell that I really wanted to be a top gymnast.

The USA Gymnastics Junior Olympic program, which my Roseville gym and so many other gyms throughout the nation were a part of, and which is now called the USAG Development Program, is divided into Levels 1 through 10. Levels 1 through 3 are for beginners, Levels 4 through 6 are for advanced gymnasts, and Levels 7 through 10 are the most competitive. When gymnasts have been competing at Level 10 for a while, they may pursue opportunities to qualify for elite-level gymnastics.

LEVELING UP

Curious about which skills are required at each level of the Development Program? Check out **https://gymnasticshq .com/gymnastics-levels/** for a comprehensive and up-to-date guide!

And if you don't recognize some of the skills mentioned there, the glossary of gymnastics terms found on page 170 of this book will define them for you.

When I was six years old, I was in Level 5 with the other girls my age. But the coaches observed that I had a lot more power and was developing skills faster than the rest of the group, so they began training me to do Level 7 skills. On bars, for instance, I was working on incorporating a giant into my routine, which is a really difficult skill for a lot of people to learn. It's where you rotate 360 degrees around one of the bars with your body in a fully extended position. On beam, you had to be able to do a series such as a back walkover, back walkover or a back walkover, back handspring. My beam series for Level 7 was actually a step up from that. It included a back handspring, back handspring, which was considered a very impressive series for that level. I was flipping backward twice in a row, touching my hands to the beam midway through each flip.

Most days, before practice, my friends were on the other side of the gym jumping around on the trampoline while I was doing extra workouts by myself. I felt like I was missing out on some of the fun. It was the first time

I got a sense of the sacrifices I would have to make to be successful. I wanted to be with them, but I wanted to learn Level 7 more.

Around that same time, the coaches pulled my parents aside and suggested that I move to another gym, which was known for developing athletes who competed quite successfully at the Junior Olympics, the highest competition in the developmental program. The gym they suggested was Twin City Twisters (also called TCT) in Champlin, Minnesota. TCT had an amazing reputation, and my parents believed that the coaches there could help me fulfill my potential. The one catch was that this new gym was a forty-minute drive from my home. We decided to make the leap anyway.

Once we had the perfect gym, we had to find the perfect school. The one I was enrolled in finished at four o'clock each day, but I needed to find one that ended earlier because practice initially ran from 2:30 to 6:30 p.m. during the school year and from 8:30 a.m. to 1:30 p.m. during the summer, with hours added as I got more advanced.

Luckily, by the time I was in second grade, we found that school (shout-out to Parkview Center School!). Their day ended at two, but I was permitted to leave after lunch at one. The only snag with Parkview was that when the time ultimately came, they would not allow me to take off to compete on behalf of the United States at international events. So we looked for a loophole. Apparently, you could be absent from school for family reunions . . . Let's just say I had *a lot* of "family get-togethers."

Eventually, I had to take online courses to make up for the classes I missed, and there was no real opportunity to make new friends there, but I was happy in the gym and that was all that mattered to me.

I remember my first day at TCT like it was yesterday. My mom got lost on the way there, so we were late to practice. As we pulled into the parking lot, the girls were already taking a morning run around the pond. I didn't have tennis shoes, but that didn't stop me from racing out of the car and joining them barefoot. I'm pretty sure I came in first. The coaches had to be thinking, *This girl really wants to be here!* And I did. All my loved ones knew it, and they literally went the extra mile to make it happen. Since my parents worked during the day, my aunt would pick me up from school in the afternoon to get me to practice on time. When she wasn't available, I'd carpool, or my parents would hire a driver (usually a friend of the family or a relative, but always someone we knew well). Once my brothers got their licenses, they would take me.

In the evenings, it was my parents' turn to pick me up. They would make sure I did my homework during the car ride home and while I waited for them to prepare dinner. Then I'd eat, relax a little, and be in bed by nine o'clock. Even the school bus driver did his part. We lived on a cul-de-sac at the end of a long road, and I can't count the number of times he waited a little longer for me to make it up that street each morning by seven so I could repeat the cycle of school, practice, and sleep all over again.

I did TOPS training in the first weeks after arriving at TCT. TOPS is an education program run by USA Gymnastics that helps the organization identify and progress promising young female gymnasts. (The name, by the way, stands for Talent Opportunity Program.) When you participate, you are evaluated on your physical abilities at the state and regional level, then you are given direction about what areas you need to work on to excel. TOPS is considered the gateway into the elite scene.

Truthfully, I struggled with the program. It was very intense. I didn't have the patience at age seven to do what I was being asked to do. I didn't like working on keeping my legs straight; I wanted to flip one more time. I wanted to move on and try something harder more than I wanted to *look* perfect.

Because of my ambition to always learn something new, I moved up the levels pretty quickly at TCT, just as I had at my Roseville gym. I would watch the girls in the levels ahead of me and try to match their skills.

I used to do something similar with my older brothers. When we were growing up, I would try to do everything Steve, Sam, and Danny did. If they were riding bikes or scooters, or were pogo sticking, I was right behind them. When we went to Turtle Lake, where my grandma had a cabin, and they went fishing with my cousins and uncles, I wanted to catch sunfish and catfish with them too. My whole family also loved going to Twins games together, so one summer when my brothers joined baseball teams of their own, I joined a soft-ball team as well. Why wouldn't I level up at the gym too? Following the example of people more experienced than me is how I always stretched and grew.

In time, I would surpass the girls at one level and move on to the next. Before I knew it, most of my friends at the gym were five or more years older than me.

Between the ages of seven and ten, I was having private practices with the founder of TCT, Mike Hunger. We'd work on the more difficult skills together for each of the four apparatuses involved in gymnastics: vault, uneven bars, balance beam, and floor. During the summer months, I began doing two-a-days. That's when we would practice for five hours, take a break, and come back for two more hours.

I also added dance practice to my workouts to improve my floor and beam. It really helped my beauty, specifically my toe point and my leg straightening. I was beginning to understand the importance of working on my form. If I was going to go as far as I hoped to go in gymnastics, I couldn't just rush to learn new and more difficult skills; I had to perfect them right down to the tiniest detail. Even with that level of attention, I was still moving up the ladder quickly.

After spending a year at Level 7, I was at Level 8 for just one meet before moving on to Level 9. I remember having so much fun learning my shoot over on bars (the skill that gets you from the high bar to the low bar on the unevens); my back handspring, back layout series on beam (a back handspring followed by a backward flip in which your body remains straight); my Yurchenko full on vault (a vault with a round-off back handspring entry); and my double back (two consecutive backward somersaults) on floor. There was always a new skill at the next level that caught my attention.

By the time I was ten years old, I had risen to Level 10. It's practically unheard of for someone so young to reach that pinnacle. Most girls who attain that level are seniors in high school who have been accepted to Division I colleges on scholarship.

Family friends used to have a hard time comprehending just how advanced my skills were. They had no frame of reference, so they would ask my parents if they thought I would compete in high school gymnastics someday. My parents would have to explain to them that by the time I was ten years old, I had already earned the equivalent of my high school letter jacket.

During this time, I loved every minute I spent in the gym. That had a lot to do with the tone my coach Mike set. He knew exactly how to motivate each girl on the team, and he used that knowledge to make us better all the time. From my earliest days at TCT, he seemed to appreciate the fact that I could never sit still. It was an energy and enthusiasm he enjoyed working with. When he saw me pushing myself, he knew he could push me too.

He understood that I responded best to challenges, so he sometimes used reverse psychology on me. He would say things like, "You know, Maggie, you're too young. You probably won't be able to do this yet." And sure enough, later that day, I nailed the new skill he sneakily got me to try.

Mike recognized that I was super competitive, but I think he also understood that even though I set out to do all the moves the older girls did with the intention of doing them better, what I really wanted to do was learn more, do more, and be better than I was five minutes ago. Their example just set new benchmarks for me to reach and exceed. It wasn't so much about beating them as it was about improving my skills every chance I got so that I could someday be the very best in the world.

One time, Mike used his Jedi mind tricks to get us to perfect one of the hardest release moves there is on bars. He believes that sometimes kids can learn as much by *playing* at gymnastics as they can by *working* at gymnastics. So, on Saturday mornings he would schedule extra workouts that were less structured than our weekday workouts. We could pretty much try new things and have fun. On one of those Saturdays, a girl in my group caught a Tkatchev in the bar pit for the very first time. That's the skill where you fly backward over the bar before regrasping it. Several of us had only ever done this in the safety of the channel bar and were excited to try it without a spot in the bar pit too. Each time one of us did it successfully, we called out, "Look, Mike, I did it!" Instead of jumping on board and getting excited with us, he just said, "Well, where's the next one? Why didn't you catch it and go right into a second one?" After that, it was game on. Three of us in the gym were really eager to take up the challenge. There was Mike's daughter Bree Hughes, who was thirteen years old at the time; Jessie DeZiel, who was also thirteen; and me. I'm pretty sure I was just ten years old then. Each of us did two Tkatchevs in a row, then three in a row, then four. By midafternoon, all of us had managed to do seven in a row. But I'm proud to say that I won the contest that day with eleven consecutive Tkatchevs! I don't know how I made the last four without scraping my butt on the bar, but I did it.

Mike also used a quote jar to help keep us inspired. He kept it above the radio in the gym. At the end of practice a couple of times a week, he would take it down from the ledge, gather us all together, and ask who had a birthday coming up. Those girls with approaching birthdays would get to pull a slip of paper from the jar and read what was written on it aloud. Then Mike would tell us a story related to the message of the quote or we would just talk about how it applied to us. The wonderful thing about the quote jar is that no matter what happened at practice that day, good or bad, everyone left on the same note. And it was always a *positive* note.

In addition to Mike, I had several other awesome influences in the gym. Two of my coaches from Roseville—Anna Lenz and Rich Stenger—believed in me so much they followed me to TCT. Within a year, Anna married and moved out of state, but Rich stayed with me all the way until I went to college, which was no small feat, as he was also a coach with the University of Minnesota's gymnastics team, the Gophers, at the same time. It was great to be guided by someone who knew me from day one. I always loved the fact that Rich could be really goofy at times. He enjoyed joking around with me and keeping the atmosphere light when I was being too hard on myself. He was always hilarious, but he did this one thing that made everyone in the gym laugh. Whenever you were learning a new skill, he'd start singing "Kumbaya" just before you'd go, as if he was praying for you. Or if he was spotting you on a difficult move, he'd shout "Fore!" the way golfers do when they want to warn you about a ball headed straight at you. Of course, we all knew he had confidence in us and that he was just kidding. It was always a good time when he was around. But Rich, like all the other coaches at TCT, was serious when it mattered.

Sami Wozney was my beam and floor coach. I started working with her when I was seven years old, so she really helped me grow as an athlete and a person. She's super knowledgeable—one of the best beam coaches in the country. She was great at choreographing my routines and rearranging my skills whenever that was necessary. For instance, if I was too tired by the end of my routine to nail my turn because my series came first, she would change the order and pattern of my skills so I was using my energy more wisely. She was also a real mom figure in the gym. When I was having a bad day, or when I went elite and was training on my own, she would always find a moment to come over and say, "You got this."

Later, Sarah Jantzi joined Mike as my elite coach. She is as competitive, goal-oriented, and driven as I am, which was great because we could just read each other's minds, especially when the pressure was on. Together we tackled endless challenges, faced a lot of firsts, experienced the highest of highs and the lowest of lows, and grew closer in the process.

In 2008, when I was just ten years old, this awesome team of coaches helped prepare me for my next big step. I had qualified to compete in the Women's US Junior Olympic National Championships (also referred to as the JO Nationals) and was headed to Kissimmee, Florida, where the event was taking place that year. To compete at JO Nationals, you must first qualify to the State Championships by earning an all-around score of 32.0 or higher at any sanctioned USA Gymnastics competition in the United States. Then at the State meet, you must achieve a 34.0 or higher all-around score to qualify to Regionals. The top seven athletes in each age group at Regionals are then advanced to Nationals. And if qualifying for that wasn't exciting enough, I discovered I was the youngest girl at the competition! It was such a thrilling experience.

When I competed at the JO Nationals again the next year, I was noticed by someone high up at USA Gymnastics and was invited to come to the developmental camp at the Karolyi Ranch in Texas. That's where the national team trained and where Olympians were made. We were all ecstatic when the letter arrived at the gym. Obviously, I was nervous too. I looked forward to something like this happening, but naturally I had some jitters. We never showed off at our gym, so I didn't talk much about it, but when the other girls found out, they were really proud and happy for me too.

Every camp at the ranch consisted of eight full practices. My strength and flexibility were tested at the outset. My gym had never sent a girl to the ranch before, so my coaches didn't know the type of conditioning that was required. I made it through the entire camp anyway, completing all the gymnastics assessments and practices. It turns out, I needed to improve my strength and conditioning a bit more. I could do everything they asked me to do, I just needed to perfect it—to make everything just a little tighter. We were given helpful tips, and I was told that I would be invited back again for the staff at USA Gymnastics to see my progress. That invitation would come a couple of years later.

When I returned home, I continued at Level 10 while training to become elite at the same time. That meant a lot more one-on-one sessions and extra hours in the gym. It also meant doing something I didn't love to do. A lot of girls learn new skills step-by-step. They will do drill after drill to get each stage right. I approached things differently. My coach Sarah would always say that I was a trickster. I have really good body awareness and a strong air sense, meaning that I always seem to know exactly where my body is as I flip through the air. Because of this, I could learn a new skill just by trying it. Even if I wasn't ready for that skill, I would somehow find a way to do it. But to get a skill tighter, straighter, or higher, I was going to have to do some more drill work.

Because I thrived when I was with the other girls, trying to do all the cool skills they were doing, elite training was difficult at first. I was on my own. No one else at my gym had ever done what I was doing, so there was no one to follow.

* * *

In the same way that TCT is the best gym in the country for Junior Olympics (Levels 4–10), there were other gyms that were thought to be best at producing elites. Among them were World Olympic Gymnastics Academy (WOGA), Chow's Gymnastics & Dance, and Texas Dreams. We briefly considered them, but I knew in my heart, and my parents did too, that my coaches could learn how the elite world works with me, and that they were the absolute right people to help me become the world champion and national team member I was striving to be. Besides, my entire extended family lived in Minnesota, and I loved being around them. I couldn't even think about moving out of state at the time. The decision to stay at TCT was unanimous.

Once I embraced the long hours and sacrifices that came with the territory, I started to flourish. My coaches and I spent the second practice of each day during the summer months working almost exclusively on my form. Incorporating dance into my training, as well as doing all the necessary conditioning and drill work, made all the difference. Locking down those subtle details led to even better scores at meets.

HOW ROUTINES ARE SCORED IN DIFFERENT COMPETITIONS

There are various leagues to compete for these days. The leagues include: USA Gymnastics (our national governing body), National Gymnastics Association (NGA), United States Association of Independent Gymnastics Clubs (USAIGC), and Amateur Athletic Union (AAU). Most of these leagues compete Levels 1 through 10, Compulsory, and Xcel levels. (I, as you know, competed Levels 1 through 10 of the USA Gymnastics program before moving on to Elite.) Routines on each apparatus are composed of Special Requirements, Value Parts, and Maximum Difficulty. Gymnasts are scored on the **composition**, **difficulty**, and **execution** of their routine.

For composition, the judges are looking to be sure the routine has all the Special Requirements, Value Parts, and at some levels Connective bonus(es) and Difficulty bonus(es) to calculate your start value. For instance, if a skill required at your level has been omitted from your routine, that will result in a lower start value, resulting in a lower score. When your routine has all the necessary components and all your requirements are done successfully, your start value is a 10.0. At Level 10, you can even go as high as a 10.1.

For difficulty, the judges are guided in their scoring by a resource called the Code of Points. This code groups skills into categories called Value Parts, such as A, B, C, D, and E skills. A skills are worth .1, B skills are worth .3, and C skills are worth .5. In Level 10, doing a D skill will earn you .1 and an E skill will earn you .2 in what they call Difficulty bonus. These value parts are used to make connections for Connection bonus starting in Level 9.

For execution, a deduction is made for every flaw or mistake that occurs in your routine. A few of the more common reasons for deductions are flexed feet, bent arms and legs, head and body positioning, steps on landings, and falls. These deductions are regulated in the Code of Points by using a scale of "flat" and "up to" deductions. Artistry, presentation, and dynamics are also observed and subject to deductions on beam and floor. Amplitude, expression, confidence, and personal style are also considerations.

The leagues offer different levels of competitions. Most start at a level called an Invitational Competition. At this meet you will compete to qualify into the State Championship. At the State Championship, you qualify to Regional Championships, then at some levels to National Championships. It is a huge accomplishment to keep advancing! It gets harder as your competition gets harder. I feel the scores from the judges get a little tougher, as they have to really evaluate great gymnastics at Championships. It all comes down to the little mistakes!

At most Invitational meets, two judges do the scoring. Each judge scores the routine on their own, and the gymnast's final mark becomes the average of both of those scores. At Championship competitions, you will most likely see a panel of four judges. In this case, the highest and the lowest scores are thrown out and the two middle scores are averaged. Judges must stay within a specific range of points. If the scoring is not within that range, a conference is called to discuss the difference.

In 2011, when I was thirteen years old and in my last year at Level 10, I competed nationally in the Nastia Liukin Cup, my fourth JO National Championships, the Elite Qualifier, and the American Classic. Each of these competitions was exciting in its own way. The 2008 Olympic all-around champion and five-time Olympic medalist Nastia Liukin partnered with USA Gymnastics in 2010 to host an annual meet in her name. The Nastia Liukin Cup is considered a very prestigious event for Level 10 gymnasts. To qualify you must compete at one of several designated invitational competitions. Your all-around performance at these invitationals determines if you progress to the Cup.

As for the Elite Qualifier, the name of the event speaks for itself. Every year certain meets are classified as events where, if you achieve the required compulsory and optional scores, you can qualify for elite-level status. The American Classic is one such qualification competition. It is typically a sponsored event, so in any given year, the event may bear a different sponsor's name.

I had standout performances at the JO competition and the Elite Qualifiers in particular. I placed first in bars and beam, second in the all-around and vault, and third in floor at the JOs. And during the Elite Qualifier, I placed first in all-around and vault, second on bars, third on beam, and fifth on floor. I definitely felt like I was on my way.

QUALIFYING FOR ELITE

Want to know how a gymnast qualifies for elite? The path to achieving junior and senior elite level status is detailed at **https://static.usagym.org/PDFs/Women/ElitePre -Elite/23elitechart.pdf**.

Whether you are a gymnast, a spectator, or die-hard fan, this resource provides a glimpse of what it takes to make it to the top.

By the way, once you do qualify for Elite, here is how scoring at those competitions works.

HOW ROUTINES ARE SCORED AT ELITE COMPETITIONS

Elite scoring is similar to scoring for competitions within the Junior Olympic program described earlier, with a few differences:

In the elite world, there are still a set number of skills or elements on each apparatus that must be included in your routine, but they are called **element group requirements**.

The **difficulty score** takes the place of the start value, and it is calculated by totaling the values of the ten most difficult skills, including the dismount, as outlined in the section of the FIG Code of Points that applies to elites.

A separate **connection value** is awarded when the gymnast successfully executes certain skills in succession on each of the following apparatuses: beam, bars, and floor.

Two separate panels play a part in determining the final score.

An **A panel**, consisting of two judges, arrives at the **difficulty score**. They each come to their own scores, confer with the other, and reach a consensus if the scores are different.

A **B panel**, consisting of six judges, arrives at the **execution score.** Working from the starting point of 10 and deducting points for errors or faults in technique, execution, and artistry/composition, each judge comes to their own scores. The highest and lowest of these scores are dropped, and the remaining four scores are averaged to arrive at the final execution score.

Finally, deductions for neutral errors, such as running overtime on a routine, are subtracted from the sum of the difficulty and execution scores to arrive at the gymnast's **total score**.

When we are very young and hold big dreams in our hearts, innocence and optimism can lead us to believe that these dreams will somehow be magically fulfilled. Success in my early years happened with dizzying speed. It did feel magical at times. I had innate skills, it's true. Gymnastics always came to me easily and intuitively. But this was only the beginning of my journey. I was coming to see how relentless work and personal drive would play a huge role in honing my skills and helping me to fulfill my goal of becoming a champion one day.

CHAPTER TWO
STRENGTH

Where there is no struggle, there
is absolutely no progress.

—ERIC THOMAS

When you look at female gymnasts, you might not know how strong we are. Our sport is known for its elegance. Our small size can also be deceptive. But from the time we step foot in the gym, we are always strength training and conditioning for a reason: We are constantly moving our own body weight around. While other athletes are throwing balls in the air, we're tossing *ourselves* in the air. I'm talking our full weight of flesh, muscle, and bone. (And that's not counting the emotional weight of wanting to do really well in competition!) It can add up to a lot of wear and tear on our tendons and joints. That's why you rarely meet an elite gymnast who hasn't had a long list of injuries.

I had so many, a boy at school once asked me, "Did you get hit by a truck or something?!" I had walked into my eighth-grade orientation with a crutch under one arm, a brace around my knee, and a cast on the other arm. It never occurred to him that all this could happen on the uneven bars or on a balance beam. I laughed and just owned my bumps, bruises, and broken bones. It wasn't a freak accident that I was in this condition; it was hard work!

Sometimes my injuries came in waves, especially when I was going through growth spurts. The tissue at the ends of the long bones in your arms and legs is most susceptible to injury then. These tissues, called growth plates, basically hold space for your bones to grow. They stay soft until your bones are finally mature, then they harden and fuse to the bone, adding an extra layer of protection from injury. If you've been involved in sports from a young age like I have, I'm sure you've heard the expression "Your growth plates are closing up." That's what this means.

When I was thirteen years old and just getting used to the changes in my body after a significant growth spurt, I had a ton of injuries. It was a really difficult time in my gymnastics career.

First, I had pain in my elbow, which developed because of overuse. It was so bad during the JO Nationals in May of 2011 that I had to be treated on the spot by Larry Nassar, who was the USA Gymnastics medical coordinator at the time. He moved me to a room where other physicians were attending to athletes, and he gave me acupuncture treatment to help lessen my discomfort. When my parents met him sometime later, they had the same first impression I did: He seemed like a kind and capable doctor. Ultimately, I would get to know a different side of Larry, but our first meeting was fine, probably because there were so many people around.

When I was still experiencing pain in the days and weeks after the acupuncture treatment, I followed up with doctors closer to home. That's when I went to Summit Orthopedics in the Minneapolis–St. Paul area and met Dr. Andrew Thomas. It turns out I had a bone bruise (also known as a stress fracture) under the cartilage right at the radiocapitellar joint. That's the joint that allows the forearm to rotate so your hand can be turned palm up or palm down. It's a pretty important motion in gymnastics, especially when you train in bars and vault. Thankfully, Dr. Thomas was able to successfully treat me for that injury without surgery.

However, 2011 didn't get much better after that event. As my elbow was healing, I tore my hamstring right off the bone. It took months to mend. I was so frustrated the whole time I was healing because I had started to grasp what it takes to be the best in this sport, and I wasn't able to put in the time or practice that was necessary to get there while I was still rehabbing.

When I finally recovered from both my hamstring and my elbow injuries, and was happily learning new skills again, I had another setback. I rolled my ankle and fractured my fibula. That's the long bone attached to the shinbone. It's what stabilizes your lower leg and really impacts your ankle's range of motion. I had worked so hard to get into shape after all my other injuries, I couldn't believe that I was being sidelined again. But I followed my doctor's orders and took the appropriate time off.

Once I was back on my feet, I qualified for the elite level. It was such a big accomplishment for me, not only because I did it while overcoming all these physical obstacles, but because I faced so many other challenges as well. I tried to qualify for elite level about three times before I made it because there was so much my coaches and I didn't know about the process. During my first attempt, I remember thinking I did such a good floor routine, but then when my score came up, I only got something like a 7.0. We were so confused until we realized I did the wrong routine. Another time, I didn't include a necessary skill. I felt as if we were always trying to figure out what the right routines were. By the last try, I was pretty confident in myself because I had done the work, I had done the numbers, and I had gone through all the ups and downs of not qualifying before. It was such a long time coming that when I did finally succeed, we were all ecstatic.

Being an elite gymnast means you have successfully completed the USA Gymnastics Junior Olympic program, and in addition to being able to qualify for higher-level domestic competitions, you are now also eligible to qualify for international events. To help put this achievement in perspective, of the more than 68,000 young girls and women participating in the program, only 80 or so make it to elite.

Now that I had reached this goal, I was really looking forward to finally showing everyone what I could do at the Visa Championships in August of that same year. It was not only going to be my first meet as an elite gymnast, but this competition was also going to be held in my home state of Minnesota. All my friends and family members were going to be there. What's more, I was headlining the event along with the legendary Kerri Strug. I wasn't born yet when she and her Magnificent Seven teammates competed at the 1996 Olympics, but while I was growing up, I watched videos of them on YouTube. I was over the moon just thinking about the two of us signing autographs for the crowds on the mall together a few days before the competition.

Then, during the first day of training, a horrible thing happened. I dislocated my kneecap. I was absolutely devastated. The thought *Why me? Why now?* rang through my head. It was inconceivable. Instead of competing, I had to watch, seated beside all the people who came to see me. It was a powerful lesson in handling disappointment gracefully. Every wise thing I had ever heard or read about rising above challenges came flooding back to me, giving me the composure necessary to get through this disappointment. I joined my loved ones in the stands, and we all made the best of an awful situation by cheering for the other girls together. Thankfully, I had been able to sign autographs with Kerri before I injured myself. It was a "Pinch-me, is this real?" kind of moment.

All my coaches were really great about helping me move on constructively after each injury. They had a detailed plan worked out for me so I could continue to stay in shape while I healed. If your leg is the issue, you work on every other body part, especially your core, so you don't ever regress or lose an ounce of the performance edge you've been working so hard to achieve. Whenever I was injured, I would condition the whole time, working on my flexibility so I could come back stronger than before. Every single day I'd arrive at the same time as my teammates, and I'd complete the different strength exercises my coaches had developed for me. It was definitely difficult watching the other girls get better and better. I wanted to do all those skills too. Conditioning is, for sure, the least fun activity in gymnastics. But I refused to be demoralized. I think the whole experience made me a stronger person. Watching the other girls' progress motivated me to rebound quickly so I could get on with improving my own gymnastics abilities.

Unfortunately, the injuries didn't stop there. During that recovery period, the pain in my elbow came back. It turned out I had OCD. No, not obsessive-compulsive disorder. OCD, or osteochondritis dissecans, is a joint condition. When blood can't flow freely to a bone because of repeated microtraumas, part of that bone, and/or the cartilage covering it, can die and break off. This can hamper your joint's movement. While problems with elbow cartilage are fairly common in young athletes, injuries to the cartilage at the radial head, where mine occurred, were almost unheard of. An arthroscopy revealed that the damage was pretty bad. It wasn't possible to go in and repair the cartilage, so it had to be removed surgically through a radical procedure.

The first doctor I saw told me that it would be career-ending. Truthfully, many of the injuries gymnasts sustain would be debilitating for the average person, but I was otherwise in peak physical condition, so I was definitely not going to settle for that prognosis. I searched for another doctor right away. I was determined to prove the first one wrong. That's when I met Dr. Robert Anderson. Although he agreed with the first doctor that the injury put my career in a "precarious and perilous place"—and he was certain that if ten other surgeons looked at the same set of circumstances, they would likely say my chances of returning to competition were slim due to the severity, extent, and location of the damage—he was determined to do all that he could to ensure a positive outcome. With my consent, he was willing to take a pioneering risk.

A decade ago, stem-cell therapy was rarely talked about and barely implemented because it was still considered experimental. But Dr. Anderson decided to use it with me as early as the postoperative period, hoping it would help rejuvenate and reconstitute the impaired cartilage. No one knew what might happen. It was one of those desperate attempts to do everything possible to optimize my recovery . . . and astoundingly, it worked. Today this procedure routinely helps so many others recover from complex injuries, but back then it was groundbreaking. Throughout my care, Dr. Anderson continued to innovate, administering platelet-rich plasma injections whenever I had flare-ups. Medical advancements like these can really help prevent or minimize reinjury. It was such a blessing that they were available to me then.

I guess this is where I tell you that gymnasts' injuries, and the treatments that follow, are not exactly like everyone else's. When the average child breaks a bone, for instance, it's usually a singular action that caused the break. They get the bone set; they wear a cast; their parents may even take them to Dairy Queen for a treat afterward; then their friends sign the cast and maybe even carry their backpack to class for them while they maneuver around school on crutches for a few weeks. Most times, the fractures heal quickly and there is no sign on a later X-ray that a bone was ever broken. By comparison, when a gymnast has an injury, it usually results from doing the same taxing motion again and again. The damage is cumulative and often complicated. The injury typically reflects the repetitive trauma our body is subjected to; it's not just a one-time trauma. And every remedy for one of our injuries must not only consider how to heal it in the present; it must also consider how we will continue to put constant stress on the injured body part in the future (sometimes just days after treatment!). We can't avoid doing the same skills that caused the injury in the first place. And the recommendation that we stop competing in gymnastics is simply not an option for many of us. It certainly wasn't an option for me. The upside is that medicine has evolved so much in response to our reality that there are many novel treatments to help us still do what we want to do even after severe injury.

During this incredibly challenging year for me, I really had to learn how to build mental strength as well as physical strength. Again, Mike Hunger's influence was so important. He was great at teaching all of us in the gym how to deal with the stumbling blocks that are inevitable when you engage in rigorous training and competition. He modeled strategies to stay motivated and mentally prepared for our next try, our next practice, or our next competition.

Whenever we were down on ourselves, stressing out, or struggling physically, he always encouraged us to ask, *What can I learn from this? What is this teaching me? How can I get better?* He always wanted us to look at a situation constructively so we could move on with purpose and a plan.

Mike also taught me one of my most memorable lessons about patience—and it happened when I wasn't even supposed to be in the gym.

A few years after Mike founded TCT, the Summer Special Olympics World Games were held in the Minneapolis–St. Paul area. Mike volunteered to help with the gymnastics event. He had such a great time that he decided to donate the TCT gym to the Special Olympics organization for an hour or two on Sundays, and he has been doing that every weekend since then. Sundays were the one day we didn't have practice, so it worked out perfectly for everyone. The Special Olympics athletes had the whole place to themselves without any distractions, though Mike always invited all the gymnasts and coaching staff at TCT to stop by and help if we wanted to.

Even though I usually had a ton of homework to do, it was hard to stay out of the gym on those days. I volunteered to help as often as I could. There was always so much laughter and positivity in the air. It was contagious. I especially loved it when a Special Olympics athlete was finally able to execute a skill they were trying to do for a very long time, like a forward roll or a cartwheel. They would jump up and down with so much joy and passion. They were genuinely excited and happy. Those days reminded me that things aren't always as serious as we make them. The joy these Special Olympians exuded changed my perspective. I had to ask myself, *Why am I getting so upset if my routine is not perfect yet? How can I be more like them and just enjoy being able to do the things that I can do one moment at a time?* It was a reminder not to get so stressed out whenever I was learning something new and not getting it perfect right away or when I was coming back from injury and needing more space and time to heal.

Gymnastics is such an exacting sport. You have to be so focused on the littlest details. At the elite level, it can be frustrating when you can't land your feet inside the white line after completing a double-twisting flip, but on days when I was missing my mark or when I had to take things slow due to injury, it would help to remember the determination of the Special Olympics athlete who never gave up, or the one who was finally able to do what they had worked so hard to do.

I know Mike wanted us to have these kinds of aha moments. He always tells this story about the time he was coaching one of his TCT gymnasts. He watched her try again and again to land her floor pass correctly, but each time she just couldn't do it. He was as frustrated as she was. The very next day, one of the Special Olympics athletes he was working with was able to walk across the length of the floor without stumbling or falling for the very first time. Most of us take the ability to walk for granted, but this Special Olympian had been working on this skill for a very long time. Accomplishing it was a truly pivotal moment. It made Mike take a step back. He had just witnessed what can happen with enough time, patience, and perseverance. He knew that with the same benefit of time, patience, and perseverance, the TCT gymnast who couldn't seem to cinch her pass—and all the other girls who were struggling to master a new skill or get back to where they were before an injury—would eventually get where they were going too, especially if he helped break things down for them step-by-step as he did for the Special Olympics athletes. These were such important experiences for us all—for the Special Olympians, but also for the TCT gymnasts and the coaches and staff who were lucky enough to take part in these Sunday events.

As tough as the year of my growth spurt and injuries was for me, I was so grateful my gym was founded by someone who was dedicated to helping athletes grow into whole people. Because of my practice schedule, I had no time for family vacations, after-school activities, friends outside of the gym, birthday parties, or football games. Adding surgery and rehab to the mix only made things harder. Inside the gym a lot of our focus had to be on developing physical strength and technical ability so we would be safe when we were doing some very risky moves, or so we could make a successful comeback after getting hurt. Having a coach who took the extra time to help educate us mentally, emotionally, and socially was a huge gift.

Mike taught me so much about the sport of gymnastics, but he also taught me a ton about life. He instilled so many lessons about hard work, motivation, and determination, and about being a good person and helping others. I would not be as successful as I am today if it weren't for him.

I really believe this coaching style made me a better person. It helped me have more control over my physical abilities, but more importantly, it helped me have better responses to the unanticipated challenges I would experience later. It's the kind of teaching that can ultimately help a skilled athlete become a champion.

I was also lucky that my parents accompanied me to appointments with the physicians and surgeons who treated me at this time. My dad is a family doctor, and my mom is a surgical nurse, so I always wanted their input. Sometimes my coaches would come too. Having their support and having a good relationship with these doctors meant everything to me. The doctors explained procedures clearly, told me the risks, and made sure that I was fully comfortable with their recommendations. They understood what was at stake for me and always had my best interests at heart. They went above and beyond to make sure I healed properly and that I was ready for the next big competition ahead of me. In many ways, they taught me what excellent care is. It is one of the reasons I was so conscious of the times when I *wasn't* receiving respectful or quality medical care.

I would go on to have many more injuries—some at the worst possible times. But these bad breaks always reminded me of how resilient I am.

One of my favorite Twitter posts feels right for this moment:

> The most successful people see adversity
> Not as a stumbling block,
> but as a stepping-stone to greatness.

> **—SHAWN ANCHOR**

Elite-level gymnasts know about the human potential to heal better than most people. I can say with confidence, based on my personal journey, that we are all capable of coming back even stronger after physical setbacks. The same is true after emotional injuries too.

CHAPTER THREE
BODY POSITIVITY

Your great power lies not on the
surface, but deep within your being.

—ROGER MCDONALD

I finally arrived!

It's a miles-long dusty dirt road deep in the heart of Sam Houston National Forest that leads to the Karolyi Ranch in Walker County, Texas. And it was quite the journey that led to my invitation to regularly attend camp where the national team trained. I had been wanting this honor for as long as I could remember. By 2012 it was happening. I was fourteen years old and a junior elite gymnast spending eight practices a month at the ranch.

Everything you've heard about the place is true. The twice-daily practices were both stressful and exhilarating. I was accompanied by my coach Sarah, and most times Mike would join us too.

When you were there as a gymnast, and even as a coach, you were under the watchful eye of Marta Karolyi, the national team coordinator at the time. I wanted to please her with every dance passage, skill, turn, leap, jump, and dismount.

* * *

Marta and her husband, Bela, were known for being super strict and super successful coaches—and some would say for making their gymnasts look practically *weightless* in the air. They began their gymnastics training career in Romania under the dictator Nicolae Ceaușescu. Ceaușescu was the worst of the tyrants in the Eastern European Communist Bloc. During his reign from the mid-1960s through the late 1980s, sports were prioritized so the socialist regime could show the world the kind of perfectionism its system of government produced. Training was tough in order to turn out athletes whose performances would reflect well on the dictator. The regimen Bela devised for his and Marta's gymnasts was particularly rigorous. The Karolyis ultimately made their leader and their nation proud when Nadia Comăneci, a product of this training, became a worldwide sensation, winning five medals, including three golds, at the 1976 Olympics. But in 1981, after clashing with Ceaușescu, the husband-and-wife team defected to the United States and began training American gymnasts. They brought their highly disciplined instructional style with them, believing their method was the only way to build champions. And for many years it did. US darlings Mary Lou Retton, Dominique Moceanu, and Kerri Strug were among the many elite gymnasts schooled in their method.

Given the Karolyis' reputation for perfection, everyone was scared to slip up or to do anything wrong in Marta's presence. Whenever she entered the gym, we would all sprint to form a line from the tallest girl to the smallest. Then we would wait to be addressed by her. She was an intimidating presence whose approval or disapproval determined your future at camp and on the national and world podiums. We hung on every correction and every rare word of praise she gave us.

At the end of practice, we returned to our cabins for the night, too tired to do much else or even to place a phone call home, which was impossible anyway, as the cell phone reception was awful there. We were as isolated as we could be, situated on thirty-six acres of wilderness. That was intentional, of course. We were at the ranch to focus entirely on gymnastics, which is what I loved doing most in the world. Still, I was so young, I would have liked to talk to my parents while I was away. It's all business at camp. It's competition the whole time. It would have calmed my nerves about my routines or about verifications the next day if I could just talk to my mom and dad for a little while before going to bed, or if I could speak with my brothers to hear about what they were up to. I've always been a tough little girl though. Looking back, I think I handled it all pretty well.

When the training week was done, we'd take whatever we learned at camp with us to our home gym, where we practiced for the remaining three weeks of the month. We always wanted to be better by the time we returned to Texas.

A DAY OF PRACTICE AT THE RANCH

At camp we woke up every day by seven o'clock and went straight to breakfast. We would all walk there together. It was a short distance across a field. After breakfast we went back to our cabins, got ready, and then headed to practice. It was an unspoken but well-known rule that we had to be there thirty minutes early.

We'd go to the training room, get a heating pack, and then proceed to the floor, where we stretched for twenty minutes. We'd return our heating pack at the end of that time and resume stretching until Marta came out of her office. Then we'd fall into formation so she could look us over.

After that, we'd begin the elite warm-up, which involved mostly running and agility exercises. That was followed by an elite stretching routine, with all the girls moving in sync.

When warm-up was finished, we each conditioned with our coaches on our own.

From there we went to all five events. I say *five events* because the staff at national team camp incorporated dance into the rotations.

In the afternoon, our warm-up was the same as earlier in the day. Our stretching was also the same. But in the second half of the day, there was no conditioning. We went to all five events again, meaning that when we were at camp, we went to all the events two times a day.

Practice lasted for roughly three and a half hours in the morning and three and a half hours at night. By the time we went to bed, we had earned our sleep.

The aspect of camp that was hardest to get used to, though, was the way Marta and the staff talked about our bodies. They were always in search of girls with the *elite look*. They would say they wanted to see *pizzazz* in a gymnast.

I think I have pizzazz or I wouldn't have been nicknamed Swaggie Maggie by the media when I was at the height of my elite career. But *pizzazz*, as they used the word, was often code for girls who were *teeny-tiny*.

In the decades after Bela and Marta Karolyi introduced then-fourteen-year-old Nadia Comăneci to the world, the size of elite gymnasts shrank considerably. From 1956 to 1972 BC (Before Comăneci), the average height and weight of the women's all-around winner at the Olympics was 5 feet, 2.5 inches and 120 pounds. From 1976 to 2021, the average height and weight fell to 4 feet, 8 inches and 94 pounds.

When Nadia wowed everyone with her flawless thirty-second routine on bars during the '76 Olympics, she earned the first perfect 10 in history. But she also became the example of what a perfect-10 body looked like in our sport. As Bela and Marta later searched the United States for girls with this ideal body type, the age of the average gymnast lowered as well. So many little girls were in awe of Nadia and the uniquely acrobatic skills she exhibited, they were eager to try gymnastics too. Her beam routine in that Olympic competition included six flight elements—five more than any of her competitors. On bars, she also introduced the first actual "release." After casting off the high bar, she did a forward somersault in straddle before recatching the bar. No one had seen that before. After the world watched her soar, enrollment in gymnastics classes soared as well. Of course, the younger the athlete, the more impressionable and manageable they were. I know I was.

By the time I went to camp, Marta and the staff had a slightly more updated ideal in mind. They wanted girls who looked like Nastia Liukin and had Shawn Johnson's power. Most people would think, *Well, they can't have it all.* But at that age, the only thing I wanted was to be an elite gymnast, to be on the national team, to go to Worlds, and ultimately to compete at the Olympics. So I strived to be the person they wanted me to be. I was willing to do whatever it took to morph into their notion of perfection. Although I was taller than the other girls, I was teeny in every other way. I was a powerful gymnast, like Shawn. I was muscular and I was elegant too. I had long lines, very straight knees, and cornered feet. I just wasn't 4 feet 8 inches and 94 pounds—and I was never going to be. When I think about it now, I did have it all. I just defined *all* differently.

During those early days at camp, I felt like an underdog. Even my coaches were treated like the odd ones out. No one really helped us or told us what to do there. We just had to look around and follow other people's example. If there was something I didn't know, I had to jump in and figure it out. I barely spoke to anybody. The joke around TCT was that everyone at camp would find out what I was made of soon enough. I was glad my coaches believed in me.

The day Simone Biles introduced herself and asked me to join the others, I was so relieved. Meanwhile, the pressure to fit the ideal was real. When I first started training at the ranch, Marta told my coach that I needed to be in better shape (read *thinner*), so the dieting began instantly. Sarah's and my parents' response was pretty much the same as mine: If this is what the experts recommend that I do, then we should follow their lead.

I was going through puberty at the time, and my body was changing, so it was tough. But all eyes are on you at camp, and people weren't being very nice or subtle.

One day a coach put me in front of a mirror and asked what I saw. "I don't know. Me?" I said, not sure what answer she was looking for. "No," she said. "You're puffy. You look puffy. Like a marshmallow." I remember that vividly. I was so young, and that's not the way I saw myself at all. But she insisted that I stay after my already long and grueling practice every day and run on the treadmill for forty-five minutes. I did that for almost a year.

A while after that awful comment, we were getting sized for leotards. The coaches took my bust, torso, and hip measurements. Then I was told they had to weigh me. I knew they didn't need to know my weight to size me for a leo, but when they brought me to the back room and asked me to step on the scale, I did. I was reprimanded when the number wasn't what they wanted to see.

Flashback: There was also the time when I came in third during verifications.

Those are best described as practice meets where you perform on all events and the judges give you an all-around score. Verifications provide the staff with a sense of how ready you are for the season. They also give you and your coaches a chance to clean up routines and know which skills you will need to improve upon. I think my coming in third out of the thirty or so other girls there definitely surprised Marta.

She had previously been critical of me during my physical abilities tests. One of these tests includes leg lifts, cast handstands, and handstand holds. I could do all of them, but my legs are so long the leg lifts were usually tricky for me, especially the half leg lifts where you hang on the bar and raise your legs all the way up, then halfway down twenty times in a row. I would typically get to fifteen. Other girls with longer legs struggled with this too. I still maintain that there are better measures of our strength than that. For instance, I could climb to the top of a rope in five seconds flat, faster than just about everyone else at camp. But at verifications I was able to display all my abilities in actual routines. On that particular day I even impressed myself.

When your verifications score is one of the top three, you usually get a medal. I was so pumped, I was like, *Whoo-hoo, I came in third!* In that moment, I could see how proud of me my coaches were.

Then Marta handed my medal to me and said, "Maggie Nichols, you came in third this week, but you look out of shape. You aren't taking camp seriously enough." In reality, nothing could have been further from the truth. I loved gymnastics, I was grateful to be at camp, and I was working hard all the time to improve. Her words really hurt.

On another day, a coach with the national team pulled me aside just as camp was ending and offered some advice. He told me I should stop going to McDonald's on my way home from practice. I was stunned. I *never* went there. I was eating *very* clean by then; I was weighing myself daily and keeping a log of every bit of food that passed my lips just as my coaches instructed me to do. I was trying so hard to impress them. I did everything they asked me to do.

Before I ever went to camp, I was thin. I even had a six-pack of well-defined abdominal muscles. I was nowhere near being overweight. And we always ate very healthy balanced meals at my house. My brother Sam has type 1 diabetes, so we usually had a protein, a fruit or vegetable, and a starch. We never had dessert or candy. I remember on Halloween Sam would have to exchange his candy for quarters, so my other brothers and I did too. On special occasions my mom would make spaghetti with homemade tomato sauce from an old family recipe. She would spend a couple of hours in the kitchen preparing it. It was the sauce that sold me. I absolutely loved it. I would eat it as if it were soup. But I hadn't had that meal since the first day I was put on a diet.

The coaches knew I was talented, but they were persistently trying to squeeze me into a very different shape. That's when things took a turn. Food became a struggle for me. Now my coach was weighing me instead of me just doing it privately at home. Weigh-in day with her was once a week. The worst part was she made me get on the scale at the end of practice, around 7:30 p.m.

That was after I had already eaten breakfast and lunch and drunk a ton of water throughout the day to keep hydrated during practice. No one's weight is going to be accurate under those conditions. Weigh-ins are much more accurate at the start of the day.

Since every ounce mattered, I would run into the bathroom and take out all my ponytails, remove all my hair clips, and toss my headband. I'd also spit into the toilet. I doubt it helped, but I wanted to be rid of as much excess weight as possible.

Soon after that, I was also told that I needed to get a strength and nutritional trainer to work with me every day in addition to my four- to eight-hour practice. My coach Sarah delivered the news and enforced the rules, but I knew the directive to lose weight was coming from Marta. It was Sarah's first time as a coach with the national team. She was under a lot of pressure to perform too. I suspect she didn't feel comfortable pushing back. Sarah had ambitions for me that she knew I could fulfill. She just had to trust that Marta's ways would get me where we all wanted me to be.

The next day I did what I was told. My parents signed me up and paid for a membership at Lifetime Fitness. I was determined to make the best of the situation. If this trainer was going to help make me the athlete I knew I needed to be to achieve my goals, I was going to give it everything I had. I put my head down and got to work.

A DAY OF ELITE PRACTICE AT TCT

I would begin my day at Lifetime Fitness working with my trainer on strength. We concentrated on a different area each day, so one day would be arm day, where I would work predominantly on my arms; another day would be leg day, where I focused on my legs; and still other days were full-body days, which involved doing chest presses, squats, pull-ups, walking lunges, and so on.

From there, I would walk a block or so down the road to TCT. Once I got to practice, I would do warm-ups. Usually, if I lifted earlier that morning, I would just take a quick run around the floor, complete what is called the *elite warm-up*, which focuses largely on endurance and cardio; then I'd stretch before Sarah would have me do the physical abilities training and conditioning we were frequently tested on at camp. This included leg lifts, handstand holds, cast handstands, and rope climbs, etc.

Next, I would spend equal amounts of time on each event. So I would go to vault, beam, bars, and floor every day, where I worked on a variety of skills. There are too many skills to cover here, but by way of example: On floor, I did my double double, full-in pike, full-in tuck, and double back. On beam, I did my back handspring, back layout stepout, front aerial, split jump, switch ring, punch front, squat two and a half turn, squat double turn, then my double pike and full-in dismount. On bars, my routine was pretty much the same. For my elite career, it was my toe full to Shaposh, Pak, Shaposh half, toe handstand, toe half, Jaeger, and half pirouette, to my double layout. Then on vault, I was training my Amanar, and my two and a half twist off.

Finally, I would stretch, then join the other girls for a motivational talk with Mike.

Now the trainer was weighing me too. He was also measuring my body fat percentage daily. This is when I was put on an even more restrictive diet. Instead of helping me nutritionally, it only created poorer eating habits. The diet consisted almost entirely of proteins and next to NO carbohydrates. My mom would prepare and pack all my meals according to the specifications I was given. She measured everything so each meal met the exact calorie count and the exact protein count required.

Most days, my meal plan consisted of 200 grams of protein and no added carbs. For reference, 200 grams is the equivalent of 7 ounces per day, or 2.5 ounces per meal. On those days, I couldn't even eat vegetables because while half a cup of cooked vegetables provides 2 grams of protein and 0 grams of fat, it also provides 5 grams of carbs. I would typically eat egg whites for breakfast, a plain chicken breast for lunch, and tilapia or more chicken for dinner. Two days a week, I was allowed to eat some carbs. On those days, I would usually add oats to one of my meals. There were times when I was so concerned about being bloated during practice, and the attention to my weight that might cause, I did some pretty weird things. For instance, instead of making a separate bowl of oatmeal to have with my eggs in the morning, I would just mix some dry oats into the egg whites and eat them that way.

I would be in school all day, go straight to practice, and then come home to a meager piece of fish for dinner. I was still so hungry. After working so hard in the gym, barely eating, and burning so many calories, I was spent. I wasn't having enough food, and what food I did eat was not what my body needed. Protein helps repair muscle that gets broken down during exercise, but it is not a very good source of energy, and my body badly needed energy. It had no fuel! Some nights I couldn't help myself; I would sneak downstairs and grab a small bowl of Special K—a protein cereal. That was what I considered cheating.

Eventually, I did start seeing changes in my body due to this restrictive regimen. I was super lean—my body fat percentage dropped to below 10 percent. At one point it was as low as 6.5 percent. But that isn't exactly *good shape*. Somewhere between 10 and 30 percent body fat is considered healthy in women. In fact, the bare essential is 10 to 13 percent body fat. While athletes tend to have a lower body fat percentage than the average person, even female bodybuilders aim for 10 percent, and no lower, during their season; then they bounce back up to more normal levels postseason. Having anything below that for an extended period was unhealthy for me, especially given my output of energy.

Over time I developed stomach issues. This may be TMI, but I think it's important to be honest about what going to extremes can do to your body. Basically, I couldn't move my bowels—I would eat something and then my stomach would blow up. I looked like I was pregnant. The doctors took an abdominal X-ray, and the official diagnosis was FOS—I was *full of shit*! As I said, I was almost exclusively eating protein. I wasn't getting any other nutrients, and I had no fiber to help move the digested food through my system. I had to take a scoop of MiraLAX every single night. This caused an upset stomach, so I had to take a TUMS right after that. Taking a laxative with an antacid chaser became a routine for me.

When I was going through this tough time, being weighed every day and being told I was still too heavy, I began to post inspirational sayings on Twitter. I just remembered how much Mike's quotes always helped me put different kinds of challenges in perspective. I thought if anyone else was going through what I was going through, I could lift us all out of our frustrations together. Most of those posts celebrated doing our personal best; being mentally, physically, and emotionally strong; working to fulfill our hopes and dreams; and supporting others' goals too.

I have always been a daredevil. Not much has ever scared me in the gym, but I was nervous whenever I returned to camp. After all, I was in a high-pressure environment, following in the footsteps of past Olympians, and pushing myself as far as I could. These kinds of quotes and a few deep breaths always helped focus me on the fact that I was there to become the absolute best gymnast I could be. That I was there to become *unstoppable*.

The good news was that by 2013 my elite career was in full swing. That was the year I debuted as a senior on the national team. I was also headed to my first international competition.

I was fifteen years old, had never traveled overseas before, and would be gone for nearly a month.

The first competition was the City of Jesolo Trophy, held in Jesolo, Italy. Typically, gymnasts from Italy, the United States, Canada, France, Germany, Romania, and Belgium are invited. Because the United States has dominated the event almost every year since its inception in 2008, American gymnasts are quite popular there. I have personally cultivated a huge international fan base. Over the years, I've stayed hours after an event has ended to sign autographs for fans in every country I've visited. It is always such a pleasure and honor to meet them. They show me such love and respect.

The second competition was the USA, Germany, Romania Tri-Meet in Chemnitz, Germany. Although this was smaller by comparison, it provided another opportunity to compete against athletes from other countries and to show off our skills to gymnastics aficionados outside the United States. My parents couldn't travel with us, so it was the longest time I had ever been away from my family. I was definitely homesick by the end of it all.

I recall putting a lot of pressure on myself to do the best that I could. At Jesolo, I finished first with the team and I earned a silver medal on the floor exercise, which was such a big accomplishment for me. By all accounts, it was a very successful meet.

I was pleased, too, with my performance in Germany, where I hit all my routines, and where we came in first, winning the team gold medal.

In November of that year, I would also compete in the wildest international competition of my career—the Mexican Open. It was an all-around competition that was established in 2011 and was held in the renowned beach town of Acapulco. At the time, the cartels had basically infiltrated the area, so the competition was held within the confines of the very well-fortified and secured hotel walls. Each of us girls was assigned a machine gun–toting bodyguard. My parents tell me that I came home pretty much oblivious to the danger of the situation. I was just thrilled that my bodyguard also happened to be Justin Bieber's bodyguard when he visited Mexico.

Of course, my parents always wanted to attend my meets. Since my schedule prohibited us from taking vacations, they would make a mini-holiday out of traveling to one city or another to see me compete. If the event was domestic, they would often fit in a baseball game, which always made my brothers happy. If it was international, they would try to take in the sights for a few hours before or after the competition. But coming to see me in this particular event was impossible for several reasons. We usually qualified for events the day before leaving, so there was never enough time to make arrangements, and even if my parents could scramble to book a flight, the United States had imposed a travel ban to Acapulco due to the threat of violence. It was a nail-biting event for all the parents, but somehow, we gymnasts were only focused on the competition.

I initially placed second in the all-around. Roxana Popa of Spain came in first with a score of 57.350 and I came in just a sliver behind her with a score of 57.300. But because only one gymnast per country could place in the all-around, and Peyton Ernst was brought in specifically to replace an American gymnast, I was declared an "exhibition athlete," and she was bumped up to second place in my stead. I was sad not to be officially recognized as the second-place winner, but I really couldn't be disappointed with a score like that . . . or with the adventure the Mexico trip turned out to be.

Sometime between the USA, Germany, Romania Tri-Meet and the Mexican Open, I had competed in the US Classic, which was held in Chicago that year. I had always been a very consistent gymnast, rarely taking a fall at meets, so it shocked me when I fell on bars. It was such a harsh landing that when I crashed, I really hurt my arm. It absolutely felt like the end of the world to me. I was such a perfectionist, I hated messing up. My coach Sarah was as upset as I was. I understood that it was only because she wanted success for me as much as I wanted it for myself, but I never wanted to let any of my coaches down.

Since the Classics are kind of the warm-up meet for Nationals, I worried that the fall might prevent me from getting picked for that team. Thankfully, that wasn't the case. I competed at Nationals after all. But at the World selection camp just a month later, I threw my back out and was in so much pain I could barely touch my toes. Gone were my hopes of making it to the World Championships that year. I didn't make the team, so I went home to recuperate from my injury . . . and from the treatment.

I would only realize much later how diminished my body and mental focus were becoming from the excessive dieting and exercise, but more on that later. For now, just know that the message you send to yourself about your body is more important than what anyone else ever says about it. We talk so much about mental preparedness in sports. To my mind, body positivity is a vital part of having a good mental attitude. I'm sad to say that at the time of Nationals, I hadn't recognized this truth yet. The criticism of my body continued to plague me for most of my elite career even though, in reality, it's our fitness and performance that should really matter.

CHAPTER FOUR
TRUST

Trust is like a vase; once it's broken,
you can fix it, but the vase will
never be the same again.

—WALTER INGLIS ANDERSON

By now you've probably figured out that I'm a pretty irrepressible person, physically, mentally, and emotionally. I had rebounded from numerous injuries—one of which seriously threatened to impede my career—and I had also endured some of the harshest criticisms of my physique from people whose opinions mattered in my world.

Fortunately, in addition to my irrepressibility, I was born with another attribute that makes me very well-suited for the rough-and-tumble life of a gymnast. I am fearless. Gymnasts have to be. We are expected to execute some of the most complex moves in sports. Take the Cheng for instance. It's a challenging skill on vault that involves a round-off onto the board, a half turn onto the table, and one and a half twists off. Simone Biles has an even bolder variation where she adds a half twist more. Getting the height to fit all that in is enormously challenging.

There are other dangerous skills we do too. Some are executed at significant heights. That's why we're trained to take falls safely. We're taught different ways to protect our head, spine, neck, wrists, and even our pride when we land. Someone spots us as a precaution when we are trying new skills or perfecting difficult ones. We wear wrist guards, hand grips, and heel pads, all for important reasons.

But there is only so much protection from physical trauma we can rely on. Someone is bound to get hurt, as I and so many others have. That's where a qualified team physician comes in. To be fearless, you have to be able to trust the people around you to keep you from getting hurt, and to help you heal properly when you do.

You would think that the doctor caring for aspiring and active Olympians would be the best of the best. For as long as I can remember, Larry Nassar had that reputation. Adults thought he was super smart and super competent. He had all the right credentials. He graduated from Michigan State University as a doctor of osteopathic medicine, completed his residency at Saint Lawrence Hospital and a fellowship in sports medicine. He wrote several research papers on various treatments for gymnastic injuries and was an assistant professor at MSU. Since the university encouraged its faculty to serve the larger community, he became a team doctor at Holt High School and a volunteer at USA Gymnastics for thirty years, during which time he was named the national medical coordinator and treating physician for the women's team. He was often described as "a pillar in the community."

When I met him for the first time, I thought he was nice. Most of the girls did. His was a friendly face in an environment where there were a lot of stern faces.

As it turned out, the treatment I was given for my back pain was nothing like the benign treatment I had years earlier when I hurt my elbow and Larry gave me acupuncture in an open setting alongside other trainers and athletes.

This time we were at the ranch. It was the World selection camp, the one I mentioned in the previous chapter. I was just starting to break through. I wasn't one of the top three girls yet, but I was climbing my way up. I thought it was so amazing that I was invited to compete there. It was definitely a nerve-racking experience. I had enjoyed my first international meets earlier in the year, but going to the World Championships would be taking things to a whole new level for me.

During practice, I threw my back out. I couldn't believe the awful timing. I knew I had to get better quickly so I could do my routines and prove I was a contender. That's when Larry brought me to the training room where he always did physical therapy. He closed the door and all the blinds, explaining that he didn't want to distract the other girls who were either training or competing. No one else was in the room with us. He said he was going to press on nerves down there (in my genital area) that would help relieve the pain in my back so I wouldn't feel it when I continued to compete. I think he told me what he called the procedure, but I don't remember the exact terminology. Without wearing any gloves, he began the treatment. I was so young and naive, I had no clue what he was doing, but I was definitely uncomfortable. I felt very violated. I never wanted to go back there again. When he asked me if I felt better, I said yes, just so he would be done already. But nothing about this made me feel better.

I don't recall much else from that day except that I didn't make the team—oh, and that Larry was taking action pictures of me and the other gymnasts, which was odd and, in retrospect, very creepy. Sometime later, we had a team photographer whose job was to record our events.

I went home to rehab and recover and to hopefully come back stronger. I saw another physical therapist in Minnesota. Of course, his treatment was nothing like Larry's.

Before all this, Larry friended me on Facebook. On some level I knew it was odd for an older man to be liking my posts, but I didn't really give it much more thought at the time. I now understand that he was grooming me via social media, trying to establish an emotional connection between us so I wouldn't have any suspicions that what he was doing in those therapy sessions was wrong.

Looking back, one exchange on Facebook stood out for me and the adults I would eventually show it to.

To give you some context, it's important to know that I didn't have many opportunities to socialize with other kids my age since I was at camp eight days a month, and the rest of the time I was at TCT training. I never went to football games or dances, or hung out after school with anyone, except occasionally with my best friend, Ally Blixt, who I bonded with in the third grade because she was also a gymnast who spent most of her waking hours in practice at a gym not far from the one I originally went to. However, I met this nice boy at P&G, which was the National Championships. He was kind of my first boyfriend. We exchanged texts, and one day he told me that his prom was coming up. Before he asked me, he wanted to make sure I would be able to go because he lived in a different state than I did, which meant I would have to travel there. Once we worked out all the details, he sent me a gift package in the mail that included a cute stuffed bear, some gummy bear candy, and a note that read "I'm beary excited to go to prom with you." I was super excited too.

Since it was a distance, my parents and I flew to his hometown together. I got my hair and makeup done at a local salon. At first, my hair was a catastrophe, and I cried. It didn't come out at all like the picture I showed the stylist, so she redid it. I ended up wearing it down with these very pretty, long curls. Also, at the last minute I decided to wear a different gown. Luckily, my aunt makes prom dresses, so I had others to choose from! After that, everything went smoothly, and my date and I had a wonderful time.

I posted a few of the photos online and Larry responded, telling me how beautiful I looked in my gown. You could tell from my description of my date with this boy that the whole event was very sweet. But the comment on my appearance from Larry didn't feel like that at all. It just felt weird.

I didn't tell anyone about this exchange or about Larry's horror treatments, even though they happened a few times. As you know, I had frequent injuries, especially knee injuries. Every time I had a problem, I was sent to Larry for help. I hated going to see him. I didn't want to do it, but it would be a while before I found the courage, or the right words, to speak up. I kept wondering though: If he had violated me and my trust, did he do the same to any of the other girls?

Before Larry, I was carefree and innocent. After Larry, I carried around a weight of concern not just for me, but for others too. He had broken more than a basic tenet of our sport. Eventually, I would realize just how fragile trust was within the whole USA Gymnastics program at the time.

CHAPTER FIVE
PERSEVERANCE

Tough times never last, but
tough people do.

—ROBERT H. SCHULLER

Sometimes being a gymnast feels like playing a game of whack-a-mole. Every time an injury put me down for weeks, I came back more determined than ever to beat the odds . . . to be nimbler . . . to be better . . . to surprise people. After throwing my back out, I worked extra hard with my trainer, adjusted my diet to eat foods that gave me leaner muscles, and doubled down on my conditioning and strength exercises, all of which improved my gymnastics. I was so happy to return to camp stronger than before and in peak routine shape.

In 2014, I really opened people's eyes. I was sixteen years old and no longer an underdog. I was an elite gymnast whose career was ready to take flight. At that year's City of Jesolo Trophy competition, I finished first with the team and placed third in the all-around behind Kyla Ross and Peyton Ernst.

Soon I was off to the Tokyo World Cup. Because this is an individual world cup, only one person gets to go. I was so excited Marta selected me. I remember feeling extremely jet-lagged when I arrived in Japan. On the way to practice the next day, I did something I never do; I fell asleep on the bus because I wasn't used to the time change. There's a fourteen-hour difference between Texas and Tokyo. I entered the arena refreshed and managed to take home the bronze medal in the all-around behind Italy's Vanessa Ferrari and Spain's Roxana Popa.

I must admit that I was disappointed to get a big deduction on bars because my feet skimmed the bottom bar at one point, but all in all the trip was a great experience. My coach Sarah and I were traveling on our own this time, so it was far more relaxed than when we traveled with the team and the national staff. We even had time to see Japan's famous cherry blossom trees in full bloom, and I ate some of the best sushi I've ever had.

After the Tokyo World Cup, the streak continued. I was in the top three in the all-around behind Simone Biles and Kyla Ross at the 2014 US Classics and the US National Championships, and was behind MyKayla Skinner and Venezuela's Jessica Lopez at the Pan American Championships. It was great company to be in. Simone, as everyone knows, was the reigning all-around champion and ultimately won seven Olympic medals—the record for most medals by an American gymnast, which she shares with Shannon Miller; Kyla was the 2013 World Championship all-around silver medalist; MyKayla went on to win a silver medal on vault in the 2020 Olympics; and Jessica is one of the Venezuelan national team's brightest assets.

I also placed third on floor at Classics, third on bars and floor at Nationals, and first with the team at the Pan American Championships.

There was just one little catch at this last competition. (Okay, one very *big* catch.) I injured myself pretty badly when I landed my double pike on the final pass of my floor routine. (That's the skill where you flip two times in a pike position.)

Before I give you the details, I just have to say this whole trip was really strange. I was so thrilled that my dad was able to travel to Ontario to see me compete, but before the meet, a bit of a situation developed. He had no idea where we were staying since the team's travel arrangements were typically made through the USA Gymnastics office. Without realizing it, he booked a room in the same hotel where we were being housed. When Marta learned he was there, she insisted that he pack up his things and move to another hotel. According to national team rules, you are not allowed to see your parents before or during events. The administration thought it was just too much of a distraction for the gymnasts. Thankfully, I didn't know about the drama until later, so I was able to have a really strong training session.

But the weirdness didn't stop there. I had been sticking to my very strict diet and exercise regimen and monitoring my weight and body fat percentages, but the body shaming still continued. During this trip, I grabbed a banana from a bowl of fruit that was set out for us after practice and was reprimanded for that. Marta said eating it was going to make me gain weight. At one of the later practices, she told my coach that I was looking bigger because of that banana.

I personally think I was doing well and looking strong at *all* the practices. I was nearly at my best then, and I could feel it both physically and mentally. I was confident in myself. I was the team captain, so I was leading us during the practices and during the competition. I enjoyed that role a lot and felt as if things were really coming together for me. But hearing Marta's comment was painful. I can laugh at it now. Eating a banana was not going to result in me gaining weight, and certainly not a *noticeable* amount of weight in just one day. But the pressure to do well in the competition and in Marta's eyes was so great, it made me think twice about eating anything in front of her at all. Whenever I was dining in the same room as the administration and coaches, I would take the least amount of food possible and push it to one side of my plate so the dish would look emptier than it was. I would do anything to avoid being scolded for eating too much.

Once the competition began, I had a good bar routine followed by a pretty good beam routine. Then on my third rotation, you guessed it: Something horrible happened. I was having a great floor routine right up until the moment I landed my double pike. That's when my kneecap just slid out. Through sheer will, I finished my routine with an improvised dance and pose, then limped off the floor. My knee swelled immediately and I instinctively knew how much damage I had done, but I convinced myself that I was fine—that nothing too bad had happened. I told Marta I could finish the meet anyway. I was committed to doing vault. At the last minute, I decided to do a full twist rather than a double-twist Yurchenko. At least I took that precaution.

Looking back, I don't know how I managed that fourth rotation. Stubbornly pressing on to do vault probably wasn't the smartest idea, but I wanted to show Marta and the others what a strong competitor I was. Besides, if I didn't do it, the team would have defaulted. I couldn't let that happen. Because I persevered, we were able to take home the team gold. It was a win for me on so many levels.

But after I finished on vault, I could barely walk. My knee ballooned, and I knew I had dislocated the same kneecap as I had in 2011. I saw the doctor assigned to the competition and was told I'd have to fly home to get an MRI right away. If I had stayed in Canada, there was no telling how long I would have waited for one, as the demands on their socialized medical system are so high. I headed to the airport, leaving my dad behind since he was scheduled to take a later flight. Because I had badly torn the ligament that holds the kneecap in place, I had to have surgery. Dr. Christie Heikes added a cadaver ligament to mine to help stabilize the patella (aka the kneecap). The hope was that this would prevent me from ever dislocating it again. It took seven or eight months for me to recover from that injury.

On a positive note, in addition to winning a team gold, I placed third in the all-around at that meet. My dad cheered the other girls on throughout the remainder of the competition and picked up my medals for me when it was over. There are some fun victory pics of him and the team on that day in the photo section of this book.

Right after my MRI, my mom took me to Lululemon, where I bought these cool black leggings with a black-and-white pattern on them. Shopping was a nice attempt at keeping my mind off my disappointment. We both knew this was one of the most impactful injuries I'd had to date, as the 2014 World Championships selections were just ahead, and I was in contention to make the team. Leaving a competition early and then missing out on Worlds again was really, really hard for me. Having that opportunity taken away made me so sad, but it also lit a fire in me that kept me moving forward. I was going to work as hard as I could, enjoy a major comeback, and show everyone what I was made of. As the saying goes, *a bend in the road is not an end to the road.*

I remember my New Year's resolution going into 2015. I was going to push myself farther than anyone ever expected me to. I was going to completely transform my body. The changes in me were going to shout "Here I am. I can do this!" I was super, super committed to this goal.

I adopted all these crazy dietary routines. I would drink a 24-ounce bottle of water before I ate anything so that I would be full in advance of meals. I made sure it added up to a gallon of water a day. Getting as thin as possible was an obsession. Unconsciously I had begun associating success in gymnastics with thinness.

To keep focused, I started journaling. I also got a good night's sleep every night.

In addition to rehabbing my knee, I used the recovery time to develop my upper body strength. I was determined to add the Amanar—one of the most difficult moves in gymnastics—to my vault as soon as I was healed. The Amanar consists of a round-off onto a springboard, a back handspring onto the vault table, and two and a half twists in a back layout salto off the table. It is so difficult, it carries a score half a point higher than most other vaults in the Code of Points. There were other big moves I wanted to add as well, from the tucked Barani, switch ring leap, and full-twisting double tuck dismount on beam to the double double on floor. (A little tutorial for those of you who don't know: A tucked Barani is a front tuck with a half twist; a switch ring leap involves switching your legs midleap while arching your back and throwing your head back as well; a full-twisting double tuck is two flips and one full twist; and a double double involves two flips and two twists.)

I saw my trainer even when I was in a big knee brace and still using crutches. I worked out on the arm bike, then right after that I did exercises to strengthen just the one leg that was free to use. People in Lifetime Fitness kept looking at me strangely. They probably wondered, *What is that girl doing?!* But I didn't care. It was working.

I shocked everyone when I returned to the ranch. I was in the best shape I had ever been in. Everyone was in awe of the progress I made physically. I mean, I definitely looked different. It was crazy. I was super lean and super ripped. You could see my six-pack. All my muscles were so defined. My abdomen never looked so good. But more important than appearances, my gymnastics improved greatly from all the work I put in.

I wanted to stand out because the next camp after this one was going to be the selection camp for Italy—the 2015 City of Jesolo Trophy competition. Marta knew that I really wanted to be on the team, but she didn't think I would be ready by then. To prove her wrong, I went back to Minnesota and continued to train my butt off. By the way, setting out to prove a disbeliever wrong is always a winning strategy for me. I got selected for the Italy competition despite Marta's earlier doubts, and I was never more excited because I had shown her I could do it.

I had a strong competition in Italy, just as I hoped I would, but going into my leap pass on floor, I actually rolled my ankle. After I finished my routine, my ankle really swelled. All I could think was, *Of course that would happen to me. Who else rolls their ankle on a leap pass?* (No one ever does that!) But I still have happy memories of the trip. We won as a team, and whenever I spent time with Simone, who was my roommate for that week, I always had a blast. We would laugh and joke around a lot. We didn't talk about gymnastics; instead, we talked about real-life situations and had so much fun together. A bunch of us also got to go shopping. We took a gondola ride, and we even snuck a small piece of chocolate. It was such a rare treat.

During the US Classic that followed in July of 2015, I placed third in the all-around again, and everyone took note of all the new skills I introduced. I must admit it was impressive.

A month later, at the second meet after my knee surgery, I actually fulfilled my goal of moving up the ranks. Cue the confetti; this was a really big deal for me. At the US National Championships, I was the silver medalist in the all-around with a score of 59.700, just 1.400 points behind Simone Biles. I had persevered and could envision myself finally competing at Worlds . . . and hopefully at the 2016 Olympics. When you are striving to compete against the best in the world, getting yourself back to where you once were before an injury is never enough. You have to turbocharge your efforts and exceed all prior accomplishments. And that is exactly what I did.

CHAPTER SIX
POWER

Identify your problems but give your
power and energy to solutions.

—TONY ROBBINS

Sometimes when you are in an environment where there is a real power imbalance, it can be hard to say what's on your mind. When we were at the ranch, all of us young athletes were surrounded by seasoned authorities in every aspect of gymnastics. We never questioned what we were told to do. We had faith that listening to them would help us become champions. But at some point, I suspected that there were some things the coaches and staff didn't know about.

It was at training camp, sometime in June of 2015, that I asked one of my teammates if she had ever experienced anything like what I had experienced with Larry, or if she knew of anyone else who did. As I said earlier, I saw Larry for other injuries after initially seeing him for my back pain in 2013, and each time I grew more uncomfortable with his "treatment." I was really close friends with the person I asked. She was older than me and had been to national camps for longer than I had, so I thought she might know.

My coach Sarah overheard my question and pulled me aside to find out more about what had happened. She could tell I didn't feel comfortable talking about everything, but I told her how Larry closed the blinds and the door when I was in the back room with him. I described what he did—how he touched my private parts. I also told her how it made me feel. And I showed her what he wrote to me on social media and how he complimented me and told me I looked beautiful in my prom dress. Naturally, she called my mother.

My mom was shocked. When you send your child who is representing your country in the sport of gymnastics to the national team training camp every month, you expect the medical coordinator there to be the most respected doctor possible, not a sex offender. Sarah and my mom agreed that they needed to notify USA Gymnastics a.s.a.p.

At the time I had no clue how extreme the situation would eventually turn out to be. I didn't know how many girls were affected until after it came out publicly more than a year later. When some of the girls tell their story, they say they never felt they had the opportunity to speak up or use their voice because they thought they would get in trouble, or they wouldn't get a spot on the team. I could understand. I definitely felt that too. No one ever wanted to get the national staff or the coaches upset for any reason. Some of the girls kept quiet because they were embarrassed. Some were too young to know what was really happening. Others felt like if they did say something, they would be blamed, or they wouldn't be believed. What if they were told that Larry was doing the right thing? That they just needed to trust him? I think a lot of people were just too scared. Anything that took the focus off you or the team excelling at gymnastics was sure to anger Marta, and if you did that, there was always the fear that you might not get the chance to fulfill your lifelong dream.

But I knew what Larry was doing was wrong. My father is a doctor who practices family medicine. When I was growing up, we would stop by his office some days to bring him lunch. I saw how he was with his patients. My mother is a surgical nurse. Between the two of them, I learned by example how medical professionals are supposed to act. As I said before, I had also been treated by a lot of different doctors because of how often I was injured at practice or competitions. None of them behaved the way Larry did. That's why I had to know if he was doing this to other girls too.

I'm glad I was overheard by Sarah, and I'm glad I spoke up when I was asked about it. At that point, I didn't care about getting in trouble or not making a team; I just cared about doing what was right.

And now, my mother, my father, and Sarah were behind me too. My dad is probably the smartest person I've ever met. He is thoughtful, compassionate, and empathetic. My mom is loud, flamboyant, and always the life of the party. She makes people laugh easily, but she's also someone who is firm and stands her ground. Both of my parents have been great role models for me. They are my moral compass. Sarah is a trustworthy, no-nonsense person as well. I will always be grateful to her for being an upstander, not a bystander, especially because it was understood at the ranch that you don't make waves. It was good to have all their support.

I didn't know a lot of what happened next until much later. My mom and dad shielded me from some of the details so I could concentrate on my gymnastics, but the following day, on June 17, Sarah called Rhonda Faehn, the newly hired senior vice president of the Women's Program at USA Gymnastics, to report the abuse. She told her everything I had confided in her, and she also gave Rhonda the names of two other girls who she believed felt uncomfortable in Larry's care, based on what I had said. (In the weeks to come, I shared another name too.) Rhonda, who had only been working at the organization for about a month, immediately called Steve Penny, then the president and CEO of USA Gymnastics, to relay the information. When asked, Steve told both Rhonda and Sarah that he would notify the authorities. Then Steve spoke with my mother. He began the call by saying, "I hear you have a concern." My mom responded by saying she had more than a concern. She told him she had just learned her daughter had been molested and that they needed to call the police right away. Steve told her not to do that, assuring her that USA Gymnastics would handle contacting them. My mother took him at his word. At that point, she had no reason not to.

In Texas, where the abuse occurred, the law stipulates that anyone with suspected knowledge of abuse or neglect must report the abuse or neglect to the appropriate authorities immediately. This mandatory reporting applies to all individuals and is not limited to teachers or health care providers as it is in some other states. The same is true in Indiana, where USA Gymnastics headquarters is located. It is clear under these laws that USA Gymnastics had a duty to report the incident to law enforcement or the Department of Family and Protective Services so their experts could handle the matter objectively and according to their training; it was not for USA Gymnastics to look into it on their own.

Ignoring these laws, Steve Penny did not report the abuse to the FBI office in Indianapolis until July 27, *five weeks* after I reported Larry. In the meantime, Steve arranged for me to meet with a woman named Fran Sepler. My mother and I were told by USA Gymnastics that she was "investigating" the matter, which led us to believe that she was with the authorities. That turned out not to be the case. In fact, she wasn't with Child Protective Services (CPS) or any other law enforcement agency, although she had prior experience as a child abuse specialist for the State of Minnesota. She was a human resource consultant hired through USA Gymnastics' outside legal counsel to conduct the interviews.

The meeting took place on July 11, 2015. It was a strange experience. We were asked to meet on the ground floor of an apartment building in a room Fran Sepler reserved in advance. It looked like it was probably a party space for the tenants. It was hardly an official place of business. I was even more unsettled by the fact that Fran spoke with me alone, leaving my mother to wait in the hallway. I was a minor at the time of the abuse and at the time of the interview, so that seems completely inappropriate.[1]

After speaking with me, Fran interviewed two other gymnasts from national camp as well. She concluded her review within twelve days and

---

1 I would later learn that it was Steve Penny's preference that parents and coaches be excluded from these interviews. In her written testimony for the Senate Subcommittee on Consumer Protection, Product Safety, Insurance and Data Security, Rhonda Faehn stated that Penny wanted her to reach out to the other two athletes being interviewed and line up appointments without including their parents or coaches because they were "adults." Faehn did not feel comfortable about that, and when she declined to do so, Penny made the arrangements himself. I, of course, was underage, so he did not tell Rhonda to exclude my parents, but it strikes me as odd that on the day of the interview that is exactly what was done.

recommended that USA Gymnastics contact the authorities. She certainly made the right call, but when we fully understood her affiliation with USA Gymnastics' legal counsel, my family and I were left wondering, *Did USA Gymnastics hire her to help validate our claims or did they want her to help them assess what their legal exposure might be if they reported Nassar?* After all, alerting Child Protective Services the same day the organization became aware of the situation wasn't just the lawful, right, and logical thing to do; it was an easy thing for them to do. CPS's offices were in the same building, just three floors down from Steve Penny's office. So why did USA Gymnastics call her instead of them?

I still can't believe that during that summer Larry was given a heads-up by USA Gymnastics' legal counsel. They told him outright that they were investigating concerns athletes had about his treatments. But they barely told anyone else about the investigation. He was quietly asked not to attend team events, but USA Gymnastics said nothing to coaches, athletes, or parents about why he was absent. They simply offered a bunch of excuses. Then, in early fall, Larry was allowed to save face by retiring. He announced it on social media as if it were just another milestone in a long and decorated career. USA Gymnastics never even told the other places where he worked—MSU, Holt High School, or the Twistars USA Gymnastics Club—what was going on. Sadly, the fact that USA Gymnastics kept the allegations and law enforcement's subsequent involvement such a secret meant that Larry could continue to treat and abuse many other young girls, which he did.

All the while, my parents were growing increasingly anxious. They weren't being given any updates. We were in the dark about all the activity I just described, so we didn't even know that it took so long to alert the authorities. Every time my mom and dad asked Steve Penny about the progress that was being made, he told them that they should remain silent about the matter, or they would jeopardize the investigation. We had no idea what they were doing. I wasn't interviewed by the FBI until more than a year after I reported Larry.

Obviously in the back of my mind, I was wondering what was happening too. That whole time I kept thinking, *Is anything going on? Are people making changes?* But I was dealing with so much else that I really couldn't split my focus any more than I had already. There was the pressure of the upcoming selection camp for the World Championships, and of course, the Olympic Trials would be right around the corner too. I had big goals. Competing at the Olympics was the biggest of them. I really didn't want to distract myself with continuing thoughts about Larry, and besides, my parents and Sarah had my back.

So much was going through my head at once. When I think about my 2015 New Year's resolution, I still see my intense dieting and exercise as a perfect example of my determination to get into peak routine shape, first for Italy and then for Worlds, in the only way I was ever taught. But I recognize that I may have also been trying to exert some control in the only part of my life I could. Sexual abuse, at its core, is about having power over another person. I can see now that I may have been trying to take back some of my power too.

I would continue to push myself to reach my goals, and USA Gymnastics would continue to handle things badly, as would the real authorities after they got involved. But that is a subject for subsequent chapters. There is still so much more I have to tell you about the buildup to Olympic Trials. And there is still this point I wish to emphasize: If your intuition is ever telling you that something is not right, seek out a trusted adult to confide in. The situation may seem bigger than you. Trust me, my situation was *way* bigger than me. But together you can navigate a way forward, finding others who can help too if the situation requires it. As you will see, we ultimately gathered an army of support.

CHAPTER SEVEN
CONSISTENCY

Consistency is the fruit of success. The
more you do something effectively and
with a goal in mind, the better you will get
at it and the more you will feel fulfilled.

—DAN O'BRIEN

maintained a laser-like focus on my goal until the day I waited for all year was finally here. The selection camp for the World Championships had arrived. Making the team for Worlds was crucial for several reasons. It's one of the largest gatherings of international gymnasts, second only to the Olympics. It's held annually except for in Olympic years. The World Championships just prior to the Olympic Games are often a good measure of who will likely qualify at Olympic Trials. People scour the lineup looking for gymnasts who surprise them, who will stand out, and who have the potential to be a future Olympian.

In 2013, the year I was first eligible to go, the competition included 264 male gymnasts from seventy-one countries and 134 female gymnasts from fifty-seven countries, but as you will recall, I didn't make the team. In 2014, the second year I was eligible, I missed the chance again because I dislocated my kneecap at the Pan American Championships. Now was the time to clinch this, especially if I hoped to go to the 2016 Olympics in Rio. By all appearances, I was in good shape. I was super lean—skinnier than I had ever been before.

We trained at the ranch for a week, then competed for two days to prove our spot on the team. The first day of competition went really well. I made all my routines and was second behind Simone Biles in the all-around again. We both posted amazing scores. She posted a 62.70, and I posted a 60.65. To say I was thrilled is an understatement. Looking at the field of international gymnasts at the time, this score clearly put me in league with the top individual all-arounders in the world. I had brought my routines far enough along to be a real contender. I was optimistic about what was ahead for me.

On the second day of the competition, we were chosen to do only two events so we could rest our bodies. I did bars and beam and made both of my routines, which was great. You can only imagine how excited I was when I was selected for the team coming off such a big injury and such a dedicated comeback effort in and out of the gym. I had sacrificed so much. I had trained around the clock and went the extra mile in everything I did. Making the team was a dream come true. Simone was pumped too. She cried when I got chosen because she knew how hard I worked, and she saw that my commitment paid off. We were always so supportive of each other.

From the selection camp we flew to Scotland, where the World Championship was being held. I wanted to do well, and just as importantly, I wanted to help the team win the gold medal. So many thoughts were running through my mind at the time. I always put so much pressure on myself to do everything I know I'm capable of doing and then some.

My coach Mike understood that about me. He also knew that Worlds can be intense. The trip was going to be a long haul. After factoring in the one or two days we already spent training in the United States, the travel time to and from Scotland, the days needed to get acclimated in the host city, the training sessions in Glasgow, the move into the official venue, and the competition itself, it was going to be a three- or four-week adventure. And Mike wasn't going to be there with us. To help me and my coach Sarah, he viewed the videos of each day's workout from home and texted or called us with his comments.

But that's not all he did. Before I left, he put together a package to help keep me calm, mentally prepared, and fully focused on what I was in Scotland to do. The package included a card for every day I was going to be gone. Yes, *every day*! The point of these handwritten notes was to remind me that I could do this, that I was strong enough, and that I had worked tirelessly to get to this place in my career. In the spirit of the quote jar we always used at TCT, he also sent magnets with motivational sayings on them. These mantras really helped me cope with the pressures of being at such a big event. It was so awesome. No one had ever done anything like that for me before. He invested so much time and thought in those messages.

As much as the notes and quotes were great tools to help condition me mentally before the competition, they were also a great example of Mike's own discipline and commitment. The effort to write all those letters, and to select the perfect motivational sayings for each day I was away, showed that he didn't just expect his athletes to have these important qualities; he expected himself to have them too. I never could have predicted how helpful this gift would prove to be in the days ahead.

Once we arrived in Glasgow, we trained for a little more than a week before we started competing. In some ways, the training was more nerve-racking than the competition. During that time, we completed two practices every single day, which was definitely grueling. I still wasn't eating a lot. I would barely grab anything at mealtimes because I didn't want to get in trouble, and I didn't want my coach to have to weigh me. But most of all, I didn't want to make my gymnastics more difficult by being even an ounce over the ideal weight I was when I arrived. I was really teeny, and I intended to stay that way.

One day during practice I was wearing a green leo and Marta came over and told me I looked really fit. I was like, *Oh my gosh, did she really just say that?* That was a first for me. It felt really good. It meant my hard work and sacrifice was paying off.

The only snacks I ever brought to camp or to international competitions were almonds, and that was pretty much it. On rare occasions I would bring Special K—that protein cereal I mentioned earlier—but not very often. If it wasn't allowed on my diet regimen at that time, I didn't pack it. As it happened, I ran out of almonds on this trip. It was a near catastrophe. I was so hungry because I wasn't eating a lot at mealtimes, and I was overworking myself. My face was pale, my cheeks were sunken, and there were bags under my eyes. Sarah saw that I had super low energy by the end of practice, and she also noticed how stick thin I had become. I couldn't believe it; one evening she brought a little bowl of broccoli to my room. She knew broccoli wasn't going to give me a ton of energy, but at least it was something more to eat, and it wasn't anything that would make me look big the next day. I was grateful, though my body was craving something more substantial. I needed fuel. *I had no fuel!*

Before I knew it, podium training was starting. That's the official practice session in advance of the actual competition. Because all the prior practice sessions occur in a different location, podium training provides an opportunity for us to get a feel for the equipment we'll be competing on.

I did not have as strong a practice as I wanted. Floor went really well. Bars were great. But I did not do my best on beam. I had a huge wobble, and Marta was just not happy with me. I think it was nerves, which would have settled in time. Thankfully, though, my vaults were fine.

I was especially relieved about that because there was a moment during the week-long training sessions when I was doing the Amanar—one of the hardest vaults there is—and I could feel my energy dip. Aly Raisman's coach, Mihai Brestyan, was spotting me at the time, and he was pretty much lifting me off the ground so I could finish. You will be happy to know, though, that during the actual competition, I made it to my feet every time I competed. I somehow rallied and pulled it off. It is amazing what you can do in the heat of competition. A combination of sheer will and muscle memory kicks in. It's really one of the great mysteries of sports.

I wasn't the only one whose energy was lagging during training. We were all so fatigued. My dad has a photo of a few of us girls standing in front of the ten-foot fence that surrounded the hotel. We were sequestered indoors for almost the entire trip. We really weren't permitted to leave our rooms unless it was for practice, but that day we were able to take a walk around the grounds. My dad was concerned that we were malnourished and that we needed some vitamin D because we weren't getting enough exposure to sunlight. Check out the photo he took of us that day in the insert of this book.

Qualifications came right after podium training. Despite my putting up such an incredible score and coming in right behind Simone at selection camp, three other girls were picked to participate in the individual all-around—Simone Biles, Aly Raisman, and Gabby Douglas. We were told that the rest of us would do our specialties, which for me was vault, beam, and floor. At first, I was shocked and confused, and then really upset. I felt like I deserved that spot. The decision made no sense to me. Why wouldn't the number two girl be one of the three doing the all-around? I should have at least been considered. The decision seemed uncharacteristic of Marta.

I obviously didn't say anything to her about the way I felt, and my coaches didn't either. Marta's decisions were always final. I would just have to move on no matter how crushed I was.

During qualifications my vault, beam, and floor were all great. I also made it into floor finals with Simone. She and I had the top two scores. On the way back to our hotel after qualifications, Marta pulled me aside and told me she was going to have me do all-around for the *team* competition—vault, bars, beam, and floor. She also said that I would be the only girl doing all four events. She wanted to know if I was ready and on board with that. I told her, "Yes, I can do it for sure." I was confident that I would be making all my routines. I assumed Marta chose me for this so the girls doing the individual all-around could rest their bodies. She knew I was consistent and that when the pressure was on, I would hit all my routines. I could be counted on to help the team bring home the gold medal. I was very reliable. But I still didn't know why, if she had all this faith in my abilities to do all four events in the team final, I wasn't being given the chance to compete in the individual all-around and to earn a medal in that event too. The *individual* all-around at the World Championships and the Olympics provide the only opportunities a gymnast has to be officially ranked as one of the best in the world in those skills. If it wasn't now or at the Olympics, I would never have the chance again to take my place in the historical record of all-around medalists. The thought hadn't occurred to me yet that it might be because I had spoken up about Larry. I was just too focused on the challenge at hand, which was doing my best in every event Marta put me in.

My parents, however, had already begun to suspect that might be what was going on. When they arrived in Glasgow, they were told by the team staff that certain decisions had already been made and that my parents shouldn't contest them. It wasn't clear at first what was meant by that warning until the names of the individuals competing in the all-around were announced.

Steve Penny called a parent meeting one evening before the competition began, and my mother arrived early to have a moment to speak with him alone. She asked why I wasn't picked to be one of the three girls in the all-around, and according to her, Steve looked uncomfortable and seemed to be reaching for an answer before stammering that Marta mentioned something about my bars routine. My mother was mystified. My bars routine was great, and she let Steve know that.

This wouldn't be the last tense moment Steve and my mother shared. I'm pretty sure he already knew my mother is not one to back down, but this interaction just confirmed it.

When team finals started, I was still oblivious to what was going on behind the scenes. I competed in all four events. I was the only one to do so, just as Marta said I would be, and I hit all my routines, just as I had promised her. Among the highlights was my big two and a half—my Amanar—on vault. I was thrilled I stuck my dismount on bars too.

When I landed my last pass floor routine, I jumped into my ending pose and was so happy because I knew my job was done. I had trained hard and met every challenge, even pushing through my extreme fatigue. I just felt so relieved. My score in the all-around of 59.232 was not only the highest in the event and the second highest of the year, it contributed to us winning the team gold medal, which was a dream come true for me. I was thrilled. It was all so special. We stayed for press interviews afterward. It was such a whirlwind. I only remember two things: feeling like I was on top of the world and noticing just how heavy a gold medal is.

The individual all-around was a couple of days later. It was frustrating to have to watch, given how badly I wanted to be in it, but I remained supportive of my teammates. I've heard people say that if I had competed in that event and scored anywhere near my individual all-around score of 60.65 at the World selection camp or my score of 59.700 at the US National Championships earlier that year, I would have placed second and been the silver medalist given the scores of the other girls who participated in that event at Worlds. But I think it is futile to dwell on the what-ifs in life. It serves no one to think that way. And besides, so many factors determine what happens on any specific day. I believe that God has a plan, and his is always bigger than ours. If I was meant to call out Larry Nassar more than I was meant to be ranked internationally as an all-arounder, I'm okay with that, though admittedly it was hard to sit out that event on that day.

After the all-around, I competed in the floor final. Simone and I warmed up in the back gym. At Worlds you don't get a **touch warm-up** (that's where you can feel the floor you'll be competing on beforehand). You just have to go out and do your routine in the space for the first time. That was a little interesting for me, but I went out and had a great routine anyway. I earned a bronze medal, which was another dream come true. I was so full of emotion.

When the whole competition ended, there was still lingering sadness about not competing in the individual all-around, but I was also happy and grateful the meet was over and I had done so well. We were finally heading home. Our plane landed, and as I exited, I was greeted by my family, friends, and all my TCT teammates. They were carrying big signs and cheering for me. I went over to say hi to all the people I love. News crews were present too. I was so moved by it all. It was just so awesome. It was particularly great to know that my hard work had paid off. Consistency in my efforts led to consistency in my performance.

Thankfully, we were given a week off from training to rest our bodies. I was truly worn out, but I continued my meager diet that whole time because I was still under the impression that the skinnier I was, the better I would do. As you can see, whenever the stakes grew higher, my eating became more and more disordered. I had bought into this false view of what an elite gymnast had to look like. Honestly, I don't think I had a realistic perception of my body anymore.

When I think about how often I came through in the clutch at various competitions despite being so compromised by my diet, I wonder how much better I might have been if I had been able to fuel myself the right way, rather than fueling myself to reach the lowest body fat possible. I now know how dangerous it was to go years without eating carbs just because people were so obsessed with reducing my body fat that they said consuming high amounts of protein was the answer—and just because I believed them and became obsessed with the same goal as if that was what was going to make me a champion. When you are performing moves like the Barani and the Amanar, you not only need physical strength, you need mental clarity. Both are hard to muster when you are hungry all the time. Athletes need energy; we need something to burn, and that's what carbohydrates provide. I wasn't getting many other nutrients either, and that led to me being so fatigued all the time. There is only so long that you can sustain this kind of abuse of the body.

My early injuries were clearly due to a combination of repeated stress on certain joints and tendons, plus the fact that I was still growing and my bone plates had not yet closed. But as I look at some of my later injuries, I really do see a correlation between them and my disordered eating and exercising.

Before all the strict dieting and extra weight training began, I was perfectly fine with my body. I never really had to think about it. Obviously, all that changed. The scale and I weren't friends for a very long time. The mirror and I weren't friends either. Even when my body started looking like what other people wanted it to look like, I thought it was looking worse. The idea that I needed to look thinner was always in my head. Whatever progress I made was never good enough. I wanted to be so perfect for the national team and my coach. I wanted to make the World and the Olympic teams.

I was never diagnosed with an eating disorder or body dysmorphia, but I definitely think I had both for a very long time. At first, it felt imposed on me by others, but then my own drive to be perfect made it worse. The situation was serious enough that my best friend, Ally, knew she had to say something. It was when she noticed my Lulu leggings were loose on me that she became really worried.

I'm way better now, but the whole experience has left scars. When I look at pictures of me taken during the World Championships and I see what a twig I was, I sometimes think, *I kind of like how I look there. I wish I still had those abs. I wish I had a six-pack like I used to.* But I have learned to fuel myself the way I need to, and I use the strong will I was born with and developed further in gymnastics to help overcome those kinds of thoughts.

When you are good to your body—I mean *consistently* good to your body—your body is good to you. Needless to say, in the months before the Olympic Trials, I was still not being as good to my body as I should have been.

CHAPTER EIGHT
MOMENTUM

It takes time and energy to get
momentum, but with it success
and results compound rapidly.

—DARREN HARDY

E ven when you're in the fourth rotation in the all-around at a meet and
you've done great in all three prior events, you still can't take the outcome for granted. It's not over until you strike that final pose or you
stick that final landing. That's a good metaphor for what 2016 was like for
me. As much momentum as I had at the start of the year, I knew I couldn't
take my eye off the prize for a second.

I had done so well at the World Championships in 2015, I felt good
going into the new season. First up was the American Cup, which is another
one of those big competitions where people from around the globe come to
compete. It's an all-around competition, not a team competition. You really
want to get picked for that meet. Only two girls from the United States get
to go, and in 2016 I was one of them and Gabby Douglas was the other.
I did well there, though I made a little mistake on bars. It wasn't a fall or
anything. Probably nobody noticed that I missed a connection, but I knew.
Despite the error, I still ended up coming in second place. It was so much

fun, and I was really happy I had a chance to compete there. I even remember NBC Sports commentator Tim Daggett saying that "unless something happens, both Maggie Nichols and Gabby Douglas, they are on the path to 2016."[2]

The competition was held in New Jersey, so we also got to spend the evening in New York City, where we saw a Broadway show—*The Lion King*. I would have enjoyed the musical more if I weren't so hungry.

A little less than a month later, I went to selection camp for the Pacific Rim Championships, otherwise known as Pac Rim. It's another big international competition held in the United States, but this one is both a team and an all-around competition. I was overjoyed when I qualified and was picked to go. I trained the whole week of camp, did all my routines, and was named to the team. It felt really good.

That's when things kind of took a turn for the worse. On the last day of training camp, before we left for the meet, I hurt my knee on my Amanar vault. I didn't land weirdly or anything like that. It's just that I had an odd feeling in my knee afterward. As I was walking back, my coach could tell that something wasn't right.

I was going to try to go for another vault because the reality of the situation hadn't kicked in yet. I was thinking, *I'm not hurt. I'm okay. It'll work itself out.* I was just hoping for the best. But that's when Sarah came over and said, "You're not going again." She refused to let me take that risk, and she was right. My knee blew up instantly. I was done. I missed the rest of training. That was the same day we got our rings for winning Worlds, so it was bittersweet. I was really excited about getting that ring, but I couldn't fully enjoy the moment because I knew I was about to go for another MRI. I was having serious déjà vu. I couldn't believe I hurt my knee *again*.

After I got the news that I had torn my meniscus—the cartilage between the shin and thigh bone that helps absorb shock—I came back to camp and hung out a while longer with the girls who were going to Pac Rim. A

---

2 *Athlete A.* Directed by Bonni Cohen and Jon Shenk. Netflix, 2020. 50:35.

torn meniscus isn't a horrible injury, but you do have to take time off and undergo surgery. Obviously, I couldn't go to Pac Rim with the team even though I had been selected.

A few hours later, I headed to the airport to catch my flight home. I had to get my knee fixed up. Usually, the surgeon trims and removes the damaged cartilage and leaves the healthy tissue in place. When my surgeon at Summit Orthopedics, Dr. James Gannon, did an arthroscopy, he saw that I also had a bone bruise (aka a stress fracture), which was going to take longer to heal. Believe me, no matter how often you get injured, you never get over the dread of the downtime. All your hopes and dreams are suspended until you can get back into competition. Whether it's a few days, a few weeks, or a few months, it feels like an eternity. Especially this year when so much was hanging in the balance.

While I was recuperating, I was usually home alone. Although my mom left my meals in the refrigerator for me, she and my dad were at work during the day. Instead of eating what she prepared, I would just eat broccoli. *That's all. Every day.* That may be one way to stay thin, but as I now know, that is no way to heal.

I came back quickly from my injury because I wanted to make it to the P&G Championships, and I also wanted to make it to Olympic Trials. But I probably came back too quickly. In retrospect I realize that I should have been out longer because the cartilage didn't heal as properly as it should have. To compensate, I had this crazy routine where I'd tape my whole knee up so I could keep it stable and it wouldn't hurt during practice. It's always hard to get back into training and into routine shape after you undergo surgery, but it's especially hard after knee surgery. You pretty much need your legs for *every* event.

Training for P&G proved to be more difficult than I could have anticipated. I was nowhere near my peak, especially after being one of the top two girls before heading into Worlds. Trying to come back was definitely a struggle for me mentally as well as physically. I kept comparing myself to where I was in 2015. But the media still knew I was tough and that I'd hang in there with everything I had. At the US Classic, for instance, NBC's Andrea Joyce commented on my absence, saying to Al Trautwig, "Remember the last time Maggie Nichols was injured, she came back stronger physically and mentally. She was a completely different athlete. We don't know what's gonna happen, but Al, they don't call her Swaggie Maggie for nothing."[3]

I loved Andrea's vote of confidence, and I also loved the nickname she used to refer to me. It was coined by the Associated Press sportswriter Will Graves. During Worlds, he even implemented a *swag meter* to indicate how well I was doing throughout the competition. The swag meter became one of my favorite ways to measure my performance!

At the P&G Championships in late June, I had a soft return. I was pacing myself so that my knee could continue to mend. I only did bars and beam both days. The first day of competition went all right. I made both my routines. But on the second day, I messed up my bar routine. My feet slipped off, which was reflected in my score. It was not a great step in the right direction considering Olympic Trials were so close.

After P&G I was really upset about everything that happened. I was struggling with my skills and comparing myself to me in better times. I was definitely not strong enough in any way, but obviously I wanted to keep pushing my body to the limit. I wanted to make the team so badly, but my body wasn't giving me what I needed yet. Taking into account all the factors we've talked about so far—the injuries, the dieting, the overtraining, the pressure of wanting to recover in time for Olympic Trials, the Larry mess—I wasn't performing as well as I had hoped.

Recognizing that I wasn't as good as I had been a few months earlier, and that my body just physically couldn't deliver what I needed it to at the moment, was one of the most difficult challenges I had ever faced. On a positive note, I *never* lost motivation even though the training was so hard for me.

At some point before P&G, the Hershey Company, which was spon-

---

3 *Athlete A.* Directed by Bonni Cohen and Jon Shenk. Netflix, 2020. 51:30.

soring the Olympic Committee and supporting Team USA athletes in Rio, wanted to make a commercial featuring Simone Biles. In addition to her immediate family members, Simone was told she could pick a couple of friends to be in the video with her. Because we were best friends, she invited me. I was still rehabbing my knee, so I was nervous about doing too much before trials, but I loved Simone and I wanted to be there for her. Because I had planned to go to an NCAA college after my elite career ended, I couldn't accept any money for being in the video. Being flown to Texas, where the commercial was being filmed, posed a potential problem, as even that could be viewed as compensation. This was well before the Division I board of directors lifted the ban on collegiate athletes accepting sponsorship money in 2021, so my mom had to contact the University of Oklahoma, the school I was scheduled to go to, and talk with both K. J. Kindler, the coach, and the NCAA compliance person, Toby Baldwin, to get clearance. Once everything was arranged, I flew to Houston. The crew started filming on a Saturday. I did my scene, but by midday Steve Penny called and told the producers I shouldn't be there. By all accounts, he was furious and made it clear that I was not to be in the final product. I flew back home, and while I was in school on the following Monday, he called my house. He began yelling at my mother, asking what the hell she thought she was doing, stressing that he was the one in charge. He told her he was at the airport waiting for a plane and he just found out that I went to Houston trying to be in the commercial. My mom was thinking, *He couldn't have just found out. He called to pull Maggie from the set earlier that weekend.* My mom also couldn't understand why he would ever talk to the mother of one of his top athletes that way, especially before Olympic Trials.

Steve Penny always held a tight rein on marketing and promotions, as it was part of his job, but his response in this situation seemed extreme. We just couldn't understand why he was so irate.

That wasn't the first time after reporting Larry Nassar that I missed out on an opportunity to participate in a special event. Before this, *International Gymnast* magazine awarded me Gymnast of the Year. The banquet and ceremony were to be held in Las Vegas. Steve Penny wanted me to stay home and focus on gymnastics, which I did, as gymnastics was always my highest priority. But it was still disappointing not to be able to receive my award in person.

On another occasion, Paul Ziert, the publisher of the abovementioned magazine and the former gymnastics coach for University of Oklahoma who recruited Bart Conner to the school, reached out to my mother because he also produced popular television specials and was planning one that integrated gymnastics and figure skating. He had extended an invitation to Simone Biles to be in it, and she recommended that he call me to be in it too. I was thrilled and couldn't wait to do it. The show was called *Progressive Skating & Gymnastics Spectacular.* My mother instantly called USA Gymnastics to clear it, but soon after, someone from Steve's office contacted Paul and declined the opportunity, saying that I had another promotional commitment, though neither my mother nor I recalled having a conflict.

When my mother heard that the request had been denied, she couldn't help but feel as if Steve was trying to dim my light. I felt awful about the whole thing. The show got great ratings and sounded as if it would have been a lot of fun to do, but I just tried to put these disappointments out of my mind and focus on getting better.

Finally, it was the second week in July and the Olympic Trials were just days away. Gymnasts don't room with their parents at trials; they room with another athlete. So, I was rooming with Simone, which was definitely a plus. Even under stressful situations, she always kept the mood light so I wasn't as nervous as I might have been.

We had several days beforehand to practice. My knee was not doing well, but I was feeling a bit stronger than I was in the time leading up to P&G. I wasn't doing my Amanar yet out of an abundance of caution, but my floor routine was the same as it was at Worlds, so I was really excited. I knew it was a good routine.

During the practices, though, I sensed a real shift in energies. I could just tell that I wasn't going to make the team because Marta barely came over to watch me. None of the national team staff came over to look at my routines either, which was very odd. And no one asked how I was doing. At one point, my coach Sarah purposely walked right in front of Marta and said, "Hello, Marta. How are you?" She literally stopped Marta from walking right past us. She forced Marta to talk to her.

And that's not all. Marta, Steve, and the rest of the national staff appeared to be distracted while I was doing my floor routine. I wished everyone could have seen how well I did. It was a really, really strong floor routine if I say so myself. But when I recently listened to the announcers' comments about the routine again, it seemed to me as if they also knew I wasn't going to make the team. They typically speak to the staff in advance, which is how they get a sense of who to look out for and which routines are particularly promising.

There was also a social media event I was supposed to be at, but I was told at the last minute that I didn't need to be there. I couldn't shake the feeling that everyone knew I wasn't going to make the team before it even happened . . . or before I could prove that I should!

My parents were getting the same vibes, but obviously we weren't together for them to tell me what they were experiencing, and even if we did see each other, I doubt they would have wanted to distract me with these kinds of concerns. At the American Cup and every other prior event, for instance, my parents sat next to Simone Biles's parents in the section reserved for the families of the top gymnasts. They were always placed in marked seats and were miked in advance so the TV cameras could pan to them at certain times, picking up their reactions both visually and auditorily. The audience loves to see the parents of top contenders cheer and cry for their children. The network producers barely let the families out of their sight. My dad used to joke about how the cameramen and boom operators would even follow him into the men's room. But it was a very different experience at Olympic Trials. My parents were off by themselves. They had no special seats. They were nowhere near the other families. Instead, they were placed clear across the arena in what felt like Siberia. It was outrageous. They were obviously being frozen out. They instantly knew I wasn't making the team, and it seemed NBC knew it too.

At other competitions following my reporting of Larry Nassar, Steve Penny always told my father, "Don't worry about Maggie. We'll take care of Maggie. Don't worry about Maggie. We got Maggie." It was apparent to my parents at trials that Steve Penny did not have my back. Since the trials were held over the course of two days, the sponsors set up booths in the mall of the arena where they offered fun gymnastics-related activities and giveaways. On one of those days, my parents walked around that busy area between events. That's when they heard Steve Penny addressing the crowd. He said something to the effect that there were more talented gymnasts than ever competing that year, which would make selecting the team difficult, and that fans shouldn't be surprised if one of their favorite gymnasts didn't get picked. It struck my parents as such an odd thing to say. As they looked around the mall, images of me were everywhere. I had been featured in an Under Armour campaign promoting the Olympics that included video commercials, billboards, banners, and life-size posters. Madison Kocian and MyKayla Skinner were also in that ad campaign. Sponsors only select you to participate in these kinds of campaigns if you're favored to make the team. Maddie was ultimately one of the final five and MyKayla was an alternate. Posters from that campaign were splashed all over the mall and in the promotional truck at the Under Armour booth. I was front and center on those posters, surrounded by Maddie and MyKayla—all three of us looking primed for competition. Kellogg's also selected me to be in their ad campaign for the 2016 Kellogg's Tour of Gymnastics Champions. In the ad, I stood with the other top contenders for the team under a headline that read, "Celebrate with the US Gymnastics Team as They Return from Rio." A banner featuring that ad also hung in the mall. Obviously, the sponsors thought I was headed to the Olympics. With my photo in just about every direction you turned, it was safe to assume that I was one of people's "favorite gymnasts." Was I who Steve Penny was referring to? Was his speech intended to brace everyone for what was going to happen? Did he anticipate a backlash that needed to be nipped in the bud then? In that moment, my parents certainly thought so. Everything about the lead-up to the competition seemed to foreshadow my fate.

But I really couldn't think about any of the things I was noticing or imagine what my parents may have been experiencing. I just had to shrug the negative energy off and do my routines as best as I could.

On day one of the competition, I had a fall on beam, which was unheard of for me. I never really fell at competitions at this point in my career. But on day two, I had an amazing competition. I was feeling good, and I wanted to do the Amanar. That's the really hard vault—the two and a half Yurchenko that I told you about earlier. So I went up to Sarah and Mike to tell them. At first they were hesitant. I hadn't done one in warm-up yet, but when Sarah thought about it, she knew that if anyone could do it, it was me. She always said I had strong body awareness. She trusted that if I started to do it and felt it was off, I could make the judgment to change, even in midair. She told me to do a double in the touch on my first turn, and if I did it well, we'd decide about the Amanar after that. I popped a double just like she told me to. It had the height that I needed, so I knew I was ready to take the chance on the Amanar on my next turn. If I came in the slightest bit wrong—if it didn't feel perfect—she told me to just do the double. She said under those circumstances I shouldn't go for the two and a half because clean doubles would still give me a chance to make the team. Sure enough, the second turn wasn't as poppy as that first one out of the box, so I made the split-second decision, right in midair, to do the double. All my other routines were great. I was really happy they went so well. I ended on beam, where I scored a 14.9, which was awesome.

Sarah and Mike were confident that in the month left before the Olympics began, I would have my Amanar locked in again, and I would probably even be ready to do the Cheng, which I had been working on for a while. That's a round-off entry onto the springboard with a half twist onto the table and a front salto layout with one and a half twists before landing. It's a skill that's worth two tenths more than the Amanar. In the four remaining weeks, I would have definitely had my endurance back.

When the trials ended, we were led to a room where we waited for the national staff to come and announce the team members. I had already forgotten about all the weird vibes I had experienced earlier. My coaches and I were pretty sure at that point that I'd get a spot as an alternate because I placed sixth in the all-around, even with a fall.

It took an awfully long time—more than eighteen minutes—before we heard any news. In retrospect I wondered if a debate ensued during that gap. You can only imagine how shocked I was when the results came in and my name wasn't called. It took me a minute to process what had just happened. My coaches told me I could stay behind in the room and not go out and cheer for the girls who made it if I needed a moment to collect myself, but that didn't feel right to me. I went out there anyway and cheered for them all. I personally congratulated every one of them. There was confetti everywhere . . . and so much emotion.

Afterward, we got to meet Kobe Bryant, who came to the Olympic Trials to watch and support us, which was really cool, and I suppose a silver lining of sorts. I took some pictures with him. He was so nice. Remembering details like that reminds me how surreal the whole experience was.

I was obviously very upset, but my family was there, so I tried to make the best of the situation and enjoy my time with them. I asked if I could have a slice of pizza and they were happy to get me some. We even had dessert! At that moment, I didn't care what anyone might have to say about my one-time splurge. I thought the situation warranted it.

My coach Mike went up to Marta at the hotel because I think he was still confused by the decision. He asked her if I did my Amanar, would I still have a chance. I know he was trying his best to persuade her I should be on the team.

I took the plane home with him and Sarah while my parents were on a different flight. When we landed, Mike drove me to my house, and I'm pretty sure he still didn't believe what had happened. I could barely believe it myself. He recently said that although I always bounced back after disappointments, he was amazed by how quickly I seemed to move past this one.

I'm sure it took longer than it appeared for me to rebound, but getting back up on my feet as soon as possible is just part of my nature. I don't like to dwell on the things I cannot change. Some of this attitude comes from my gymnastics training as well. When you have a nanosecond between a less-than-stellar vault and your next try, you have to put your disappointment out of your head and give the next attempt your best effort. This has been the way I've coped for almost my entire life.

But the following day, another huge thing happened. Everyone who made the team was invited to a meeting where they talked about next steps and got sized for new clothes. Strangely, I was invited to go too. When I got there, I was the only one who didn't have a USA warm-up jacket on because I didn't make the team. I was sitting with all the other girls looking really out of place. It was horrible—one of the worst experiences of my life. It seriously was. I couldn't imagine why I was there.

My coach Sarah must have known how uncomfortable I was even though I tried to hide it. She told me to get sized too, so at least I would get some clothes out of the whole thing. But I didn't want that.

Later that day, I was told that I was asked to be a stay-at-home alternate, which was probably why I was at that meeting. It meant I wouldn't travel to Rio, where the Olympics were being held, but I would wait at home in the unlikely event I was needed.

At that point, though, I was ready for a new challenge, so I went into the gym to tell Mike and Sarah I was retiring from elite gymnastics. I showed them the announcement I had written and they both thought it was perfect.

I said a lot of meaningful things in that announcement, but I closed by saying that I had some tears after trials—both happy and sad. I also mentioned that I was proud of how far I had come in my recovery from injury, and how well I thought I performed at trials. I wanted to end my career with a bang, and I think I did that. The second night of trials, I had so many amazing feelings. I wrote that after I finished my beam routine, it was the happiest I had ever been after a competition. And that was the truth.

My parents read my statement too. They were also very happy I was retiring and preparing for my next chapter in life. After the announcement was posted, I remember my mom coming into my room and telling me how proud she was of me. That was really comforting to hear.

But there was still some uneasy business left for me to deal with. In July of 2016, my mom had received a call from FBI agent Michael Hess. He wanted to fly to Minnesota to interview me just before we headed to San Jose, where the Olympic Trials were being held. When my mom told him I was getting ready for trials, he seemed surprised to learn I was even a contender for the team. She couldn't figure out why this agent was calling me then or how he couldn't have known I was going to trials. Didn't Steve Penny tell him I needed to focus on my gymnastics? Was his call a case of unfortunate timing or just another indication of things to come?

Now that the trials were over, I really didn't want to think about things like that. My association with USA Gymnastics was behind me. I had to try to just carry on, and as I said then, hope that they made the right decisions for the right reasons. But since Agent Hess honored my mother's request and waited a few weeks longer to interview me, I took the meeting. I remember I had just gotten my driver's license, so I drove there alone to talk with him. It was the most uncomfortable conversation. It was difficult enough to talk to Sarah about what happened even though I trusted her like a second mom—and to talk to Fran Sepler later, whom I didn't know at all—but now I had to talk to this male stranger. The whole experience was very awkward and unsettling.

After that, I took the week off and decided to enjoy myself. My friend Ally and I went to Five Guys as a treat. I had never been there before. We got a hamburger and fries. It was so cool because I finally got to eat a burger. I can't tell you how awesome that was. Of course, I thought, *Oh my God, I'm going to gain so much weight*. But everyone kept assuring me I could eat one hamburger and a serving of fries without that happening.

We also went tanning at the lake one day. I couldn't recall the last time I was able to just hang out like that. Enjoying myself with friends was impor-

With some of the girls from
Roseville Gymnastics at a
pizza party after practice.

Six-year-old me, Level 4,
during team pictures.

My friend Lexi and me at the
Tour of Gymnastics Champions
to watch the 2004 Olympic team,
particularly Carly Patterson.

Little me, around the age of six, competing a front handspring on vault.

Me at one of my Level 4 competitions
at age six.

My best friend Ally and me. We have
been best friends since third grade.

The Pan American Championships, when my dad, John Nichols, had to collect my medals for me.

My teammates sending me love after my knee injury that day.

Outside our hotel during the 2015 World Championships.

After a practice day in Scotland at the 2015 World Championships.

My coaches Sarah Jantzi and Mike Hunger and me at the 2015 National Championships before day one of competition.

Before bars in Italy
in 2015.

Getting interviewed at
the 2015 National
Championships after
day one of competition,
sitting in second place
behind Simone Biles.

Simone Biles, Madison Kocian, and me at a photo shoot at the ranch.

Kobe Bryant and me after Olympic Trials.

Me enjoying pizza after Olympic Trials.

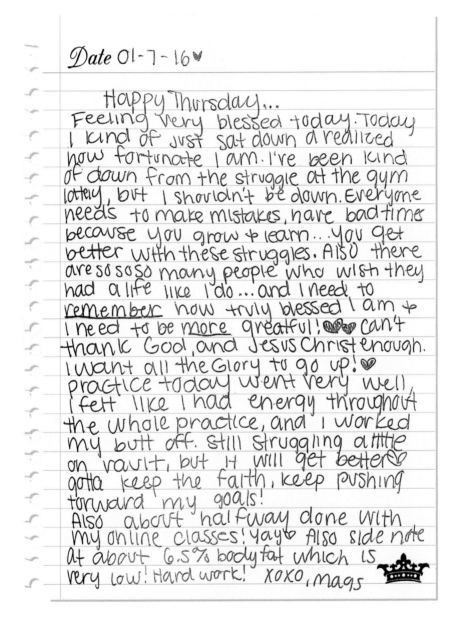

Date 01-7-16 ♥

Happy Thursday...
Feeling very blessed today. Today
I kind of just sat down a realized
how fortunate I am. I've been kind
of down from the struggle at the gym
lately, but I shouldn't be down. Everyone
needs to make mistakes, have bad time
because you grow & learn... you get
better with these struggles. Also there
are so so so many people who wish they
had a life like I do... and I need to
remember how truly blessed I am &
I need to be more greatful! ♥♥ Can't
thank God, and Jesus Christ enough.
I want all the Glory to go up! ♥
practice today went very well,
I felt like I had energy throughout
the whole practice, and I worked
my butt off. Still struggling a little
on vault, but it will get better♥
gotta keep the faith, keep pushing
forward my goals!
Also about halfway done with
my online classes! Yay♥ Also side note
at about 6.5% body fat which is
very low! Hard work! xoxo, mags ♛

No matter how intense things got in 2016, I kept positive
and focused on my goals, as this diary entry from that time shows.

Move-in day at the University of Oklahoma in August of 2016.

Morning workout at OU with Jade Degouveia and Bre Showers.

Kissing the National Championship trophy in 2017.

My coach Lou Ball and me celebrating after my bar routine
at the NCAA Championships.

After I stuck my vault and clinched the national title in 2017.

My teammates and me after we just won the NCAA Championships in 2017.

COURTESY OF THE AUTHOR

COURTESY OF THE AUTHOR

My best friends Natalie Brown and Bre Showers at the White House in 2017 after we won the National Championship.

CBP SOURCED / ALAMY STOCK PHOTO

The 2017 National Championship team at the White House in 2017.

At the ESPYs after receiving the
Arthur Ashe Courage Award.

My coach Tom Haley prepping me for my
floor routine in 2019, seconds before
clinching the all-around title.

Celebrating my bar routine at the Regional Championships after scoring a 10.0
and my team advancing to the NCAA Championships.

K. J. and me after my 10.0 bar routine at Regionals in 2019.

My teammate Olivia Trautman and me celebrating at the Regional
Championships in 2019 after we advanced to the NCAA Championships.

Back handspring back layout at the 2019 NCAA Championships.

My final pose on floor exercise at the 2019 NCAA Championships.

After my floor routine at the 2019 National Championships, celebrating a hit routine!

My team and me celebrating our 2019 NCAA national title.

On top of the podium after clinching the all-around title at
the NCAA Championships in 2019.

Me doing the Michael Jordan pose with all my rings.

tant. It reaffirmed that although I had just experienced the biggest setback of my gymnastics career, it wasn't the end of the road for me. Far from it. It's true I had wanted to represent my country at the Olympics more than anything, but how I represent myself in any set of circumstances—good or bad—is what really matters. I would just have to put my big girl leo on and do what I do best somewhere else.

That same week, I called K. J. Kindler, the head coach at the University of Oklahoma's women's gymnastics team, and I asked her if I could come to school early. After accepting the offer to go to OU as part of the incoming class in 2016, I had deferred for a semester so I could go on the Kellogg's Tour of Gymnastics Champions. That's a show that travels to thirty-six different US cities and features elite gymnastics skills mixed with modern art performance. While I'm sure the tour would have been great fun, I had a change of heart about deferring. I was now eager to get on with my collegiate career. K. J. had come to trials to support me, so she witnessed one of the most disappointing days of my life. I trusted she would understand my reasons for changing plans and be okay with me starting school sooner rather than later. Thankfully, she was really excited to hear my news. That was a huge part of why it was so easy for me to move on to the next chapter in my life. I couldn't possibly dwell on not making the Olympic team when I had something so great to look forward to.

When I was ten years old, I went to a camp at OU. Some of my older teammates were being recruited by colleges at the time, and they invited me to go with them. I remember loving everyone I met there. K. J. Kindler, Lou Ball, and Tom Haley were the coaches then and are still the coaches today. OU's trainer, Jenn Richardson, was there then too. It's so crazy to look back and think that they watched me when I was so young. They made such a lasting impression on me. I'd known I wanted to be an Oklahoma Sooner ever since then.

When I got older and was recruited by Division I colleges, my mind always went back to OU. I went on all the college visits anyway. I met with the folks at Utah, Georgia, and Alabama, as well as Oklahoma. I got recruited by many US colleges at the Division I level. Checking out the campuses at all those schools was a great experience. It was super fun. But my mind was made up. OU just felt like home to me.

When I watched the OU coaches on TV with their team, the Sooners, they reminded me so much of my coaches at TCT. I could just tell they were the best college coaching staff in the nation and that I was going to be the most successful there. They were going to grow me into a national champion. And not only did the coaches impress me, but the campus was just so beautiful too.

There were so many people rooting for me—so many people who wanted me to come there and be a part of things. I definitely felt the Sooner Magic. I was only sixteen years old when I committed to going there. It was two years before any other students in my grade were accepted to college. In fact, when the high school threw a party for the graduating seniors who were sports signees, they forgot to include me. When they realized their error and noted that I was the only student going to a Division I school, they hung a huge banner in the hall congratulating me.

I remember watching the 2016 NCAA Championship and being so excited that I was going to a championship-winning school—*that* championship-winning school. There are eighty-one college gymnastics programs in the country offering approximately a thousand gymnasts an opportunity to compete. Sixty-two of those programs are Division I. Based on national qualifying scores, Oklahoma is ranked among the highest, frequently holding the number one slot.

I also loved that OU has such a great balance between academics and athletics.

There was no looking back now. I had a new goal in my head, and having goals was always how I thrived.

As soon as K. J. told me I could join the team earlier than I planned, I went back into training. I wanted to work on college skills even before I got to school. At TCT and at the ranch, I always had to do bars on the elite setting, which meant the bars were super close together. But for college I got to move the bars wider apart. I was just having so much fun with that because, as you know, at five feet six inches I'm a taller gymnast; swinging with the bars close together was more challenging. The new setting was so much more freeing for me. Suddenly, going to the gym was a blast again.

The scoring system in college is similar to the scoring system in Junior Olympic gymnastics with some skills having different difficulty values. In elite gymnastics judges use a two-part system: one part scores **execution** and the other scores **difficulty**. When judging execution, if all special requirements are met, you will start at 10.0 and deduct in tenths of points for mistakes made throughout the routine. When judging difficulty, you start at zero and can earn points for connective value and difficulty value; the two marks are then added together for a final score. Given the open-ended nature of the difficulty value, the final score will exceed a 10.0. This scoring system allows a gymnast to make up for any mistakes they make in execution by adding more difficult skills to their routines. NCAA judges, by comparison, simply use a 10-point scoring system. If all special requirements are met, gymnasts will start at 9.4. They will then add connective and difficulty value to earn bonus and enhance the score to a 10.0. Tenths of points will be deducted for execution mistakes. Thus, in college gymnastics there is a lot more pressure to get every detail just right on the higher value individual skills.

Lucky for me, I loved working on skills that I could perfect. And I loved the idea of getting to Oklahoma and doing my best to help the team win another National Championship. I was having a ton of fun again. I felt recharged, newly challenged, and ready to embrace my future.

You will be happy to know that there is life after Olympic Trials—and that sometimes the disappointments we expect to stop us in our tracks are the very things that provide us with the momentum to move forward.

CHAPTER NINE
ADVOCACY

I learned a long time ago the wisest thing
I can do is be on my own side, be an
advocate for myself and others like me.

—MAYA ANGELOU

Before I could pack my things into my old Toyota Corolla and head south to OU with my parents, something major—I mean really big—happened.

On August 4, 2016, just two days before the gymnastics competitions began at the Olympic Games in Rio, the *Indianapolis Star* (also known as the *IndyStar)* ran a story that set into motion USA Gymnastics' and Larry Nassar's very public fall from grace. The article's headline read: "A blind eye to sex abuse: How USA Gymnastics failed to report cases."

The article, by Marisa Kwiatkowski, Mark Alesia, and Tim Evans, explained how a policy at the organization enabled sex abuse allegations to remain uninvestigated for years. It revealed that in a 2013 lawsuit, former officials of USA Gymnastics admitted in sworn testimony that unless allegations of sex abuse came directly from a victim or the victim's parents, they treated the allegation as hearsay. In other words, they didn't bother to follow up or notify law enforcement, as is their obligation under the mandatory-reporting laws when the alleged abuse involves a minor.

USA Gymnastics wouldn't disclose how many allegations it received annually, but there were records of complaints against more than fifty coaches within its wide network of member gyms. The reporters noted at least four cases that USA Gymnastics had been warned about, where coaches went on to abuse at least fourteen girls.

In a deposition for one of the court cases cited in the article, Steve Penny addressed the policy, saying, "To the best of my knowledge, there is no duty to report if you are—if you are third-party to some allegation. You know, that lies with the person who has firsthand knowledge." I believe the policy and this statement from Penny were intended to put as much distance as possible between USA Gymnastics and the responsibility to do the right thing and protect young girls. In my situation, the sexual abuse was reported directly to USA Gymnastics by my coach and *my parents*, who were vocal advocates for me. USA Gymnastics' disgusting policy couldn't be applied to me because it was clearly not a case of "hearsay." By the way, this warped rule USA Gymnastics came up with is not the way the law works at all. As I noted before, anyone with knowledge of abuse or reason to believe abuse has occurred has a legal obligation to report.

I suspect that this breaking story in the *IndyStar* was exactly the kind of bad publicity Steve Penny and USA Gymnastics were hoping, and apparently angling, to avoid. I say *angling* because two years later, in the winter of 2018, a thorough independent study conducted by the law firm Ropes & Gray, commissioned by the US Olympic Committee, revealed Steve Penny and then supervisor of the Indianapolis Metropolitan Police Department's child abuse unit, Bruce Smith, had been communicating with each other throughout the summer of 2016, just as the *IndyStar* was preparing its August 4 story. According to the Ropes & Gray report, Penny asked Smith to help "kill the story." Their determination to protect USA Gymnastics' reputation is evidenced by a single damning line in their text exchange: "We need to body slam the other sources."

While the *IndyStar* article was focused on the organization's negligent handling of complaints, the reporters did not yet know about Nassar. If at any point before or during the Olympic Trials, Steve Penny and USA Gymnastics were trying to keep me in the shadows to prevent the truth from coming out about my allegations against him, they miscalculated because my truth—and all the other girls'—was going to come out anyway. It breaks my heart to think that because they were aware of the brewing story, they may not have wanted me to make the Olympic team, as team members frequently attract a lot of media interest.

Just days after the initial story broke about USA Gymnastics' awful policy of ignoring sexual abuse allegations, I sat down to watch the Olympics as I had every four years since I was a little kid. No matter what I suspected the organization's administration did to me, I still loved gymnastics, and I still loved my teammates. I watched and cheered for them from my home. I was really excited for all the girls, and especially for Simone, who went on to win the all-around. We were so close at the time, so of course I was pumped for her. I've always had a huge heart full of affection for my former national teammates. I've never looked poorly upon any of the girls and have always supported and wanted the best for them. Cheering for the US team was just second nature to me.

As the dominoes were tumbling for USA Gymnastics and Larry Nassar, it was time for my parents and me to take the eleven-hour drive from Minnesota to Oklahoma. Pardon the pun, but I couldn't become a Sooner soon enough.

In our state, you can get your driver's license at age sixteen, but I didn't get mine until I turned eighteen, right after Olympic Trials, because drivers' ed classes were at the same time as practice, so my coach insisted I postpone them. Even though I had my license now, going all that distance by myself as a new driver didn't seem like such a great idea. So, we turned my going-off-to-college into a bit of a family road trip. My dad, mom, and I piled into my secondhand car and drove the whole way there. We listened to music, stopped for meals, made a pit stop in Nebraska for a day or two, then resumed driving, talking, and laughing. I even caught up on a movie or two. When we finally arrived at campus and pulled up to my dorm at Headington Hall, I was greeted by all my new teammates. It was just so awesome to be welcomed by them. They unpacked the car and carried all my stuff in just one load up to my new room. It was amazing to have a whole team of people there to support and help me. It's just the OU way. It's how they greet every team member. I looked forward to getting to know each of these girls and to supporting them too. Together I hoped we would strive to win four Big 12 titles and four National Championships.

But even as I was enjoying my new beginnings, more events were quietly and quickly developing that would have me thinking about the past again.

Apparently, the *IndyStar* story prompted a woman to come forward—not to report abuse by coaches, but to report sexual abuse by *Larry Nassar*. She explained to reporter Mark Alesia that it occurred when she was a high school gymnast sixteen years earlier. She had a legal degree by now and was homeschooling her children, but she had carried this trauma around for a very long time and was willing to use her name in subsequent articles if it helped. Her name was Rachael Denhollander. When Alesia told her it was not too late to file a complaint with law enforcement, that's exactly what Rachael did.

There couldn't have been a better person on the receiving end of Rachael's call to the Michigan State University Police Department. Then Detective Sergeant Andrea Munford had graduated from MSU in 1997, joined the police department after that, and in 2014 began building a different kind of special victims' unit within the department. The unit's approach demanded that victims be treated with compassion and respect. She took every precaution against retraumatizing survivors when they told their story. There was no room for skepticism under her watch.

After Andrea had listened attentively to Rachael's account, she asked her for the name of the doctor who had molested her. Andrea immediately recognized it from a previous complaint made in 2014 by a woman named Amanda Thomashow. Thomashow filed an official Title IX complaint against Nassar with MSU, saying that he had inappropriately touched her during a medical exam. But the university neglected to act on the complaint because they believed Nassar's explanation that the techniques he used were medically appropriate. The prosecution at the time also chose not to act on Thomashow's case. So with this latest complaint against Nassar, Andrea Munford asked Larry to come to the station for a check-in. It had been a couple of years since they spoke, and she wanted to see what he was up to.

With an abundance of patience, Andrea let Larry talk long enough to implicate himself. He became increasingly uncomfortable during their discussion and proceeded to lie on tape, saying that he did not and would not vaginally penetrate his patients as part of a medical treatment, when of course, that's exactly what he did.

Meanwhile, Mark Alesia at the *IndyStar* received another call. This one was from someone who would only identify herself as a national champion gymnast. She too had been sexually abused by Nassar and was calling to corroborate the reporters' findings, but declined to be mentioned in any subsequent writing on the subject.

When a third call came in from a former Olympian, Mark saw a trend and knew he and his colleagues were onto something.

On September 12, 2016, the same team of investigative reporters at the *IndyStar* that had penned the August 4 story published another article. In it they revealed that two former gymnasts had come forward to accuse Larry Nassar of sexually abusing them when they were minors in the 1990s and 2000s. The article explained that both were now adults and that one, Rachael Denhollander, had filed a police complaint in Michigan, while the other, a still unnamed Olympic medalist, filed a civil lawsuit in California. Jamie Dantzscher, who had competed in the 2000 Sydney games, would later identify herself as the unnamed Olympic medalist in the article.

Jessica Howard, the caller who declined to be included in Alesia's reporting, would publicly come forward sometime later. Her reluctance to be included in the article, and Jamie's initial hesitance to be named, are strong indications of the culture of fear that existed at USA Gymnastics even among athletes who had long since retired from competition.

The attorney for Jamie was John Manly, from the firm Manly, Stewart & Finaldi. My mother wasted no time calling Mr. Manly as soon as she read the article, and I'm glad she did. John is one of the most respected and successful attorneys litigating sexual abuse cases in the country. Soon after that call, I became the first of the 2016 national team members to pursue legal recourse against Larry Nassar and his enablers: MSU, USA Gymnastics, and the US Olympic & Paralympic Committee. John has been one of our biggest supporters ever since.

On September 20, 2016, Larry was fired from Michigan State University, but he had still not been charged with a crime.

Even more women were inspired by the second *IndyStar* article to come forward and report their abuses too. Because some said the abuses occurred while being treated in the basement of Larry's home, a warrant was executed to search his house. One of the investigators noticed a garbage bin on the curbside outside the home. The trash hadn't been collected yet that day, so Munford told him to pack up the contents of the bin and bring it down to the station along with anything else they collected from the home. Inside the trash, they found several discarded hard drives. Larry hadn't cleaned up his mess in time. More than 37,000 images of child pornography were on them.

By October, Detective Sergeant Andrea Munford and her team knew they had enough to approach the state attorney general's office to pursue prosecution against Nassar.

There they met with then Assistant Attorney General Angela Povilaitis. Povilaitis was as committed a victims' advocate as Munford. She had been a prosecutor in Michigan's Wayne County for a decade. After joining the state attorney general's office, she then spent sixteen years leading a statewide sexual assault program focused on complicated cases, including multivictim and delayed-disclosure sexual assault cases. She was the perfect person to be prosecuting Nassar, since so many of his victims were finding the courage to come forward now, years after their assaults. Assistant Attorney General Angela Povilaitis and Detective Sergeant Andrea Munford shared the same philosophies, and now they were on a common mission.

It is still hard for me to process this, but in November of 2016, Nassar ran for the Holt school board and received 21 percent of the vote. He could not stop himself from being near kids, and clearly some people were either unaware of or still naive to the truth about him.

Later that month, close to Thanksgiving, Nassar had been charged with three counts of first degree criminal sexual conduct in Ingham County, Michigan. It was in that county that Nassar treated patients at MSU's sports medicine clinic and at his home in Holt. Nassar pleaded not guilty and was released on a $1 million bond.

Around the same time, Texas Rangers showed up at the Karolyi Ranch wanting to speak with medical personnel. They were met by Amy White, the former national teams manager. Amy didn't know what to do, so she contacted Steve Penny, who instructed her to tell them that they could come back at a later date when camp was not in session. That same day, after learning that the Rangers were going to return with a search warrant, Penny told Amy to go to the store and purchase a suitcase large enough to pack up any medical forms and other documents with Larry's name on them. And that is exactly what she did. Penny also told her that he wanted those materials personally delivered to him at the USA Gymnastics headquarters in Indianapolis. Amy brought the suitcase and two boxes to the headquarters per his orders. The second box, which Penny helped her carry, could not be located later. As the heat intensified in 2017, Steve resigned from his post at USA Gymnastics, and in 2018 he was indicted on charges of evidence tampering.

By December of 2016, a federal grand jury indicted Nassar on two charges: possession of child pornography and receipt/attempted receipt of child pornography, both charges related to the computer files and disks recovered from his home. After his arrest, he remained in jail for the duration of the criminal proceedings.

By the time of his trial, more than 265 people came forward with allegations of sexual abuse against Nassar. It was distressing to see so many of my friends among those survivors. We had trained together, and we were all really close, yet we had no idea what was happening to each other behind the scenes. We only knew what we were dealing with individually. We didn't know the extreme extent of it. Just to see it all unfold was shocking. Being together as much as we were, we talked about everything, but I guess that subject was just too sensitive. It took me a while to ask another teammate about it, so I can imagine what the other girls were thinking and going through at the time.

When you look at the huge number of people Larry hurt, and how they all kept it to themselves, you realize just how lonely being a victim is. But now we had an amazing team of legal experts in place to see to it that justice would be served. This team definitely had our backs. It would take time, for sure, but in that time, I would focus on healing and moving forward. I would also focus on another increasingly important team to me: the Sooners. There was just something about being a part of a close-knit group of young women with a common goal, purpose, and passion, all evidencing our strength together, that felt super comforting to me.

CHAPTER TEN
SUCCESS

Success is no accident. It is hard work,
perseverance, learning, studying,
sacrifice and most of all, love of what
you are doing or learning to do.

—PELÉ

Some people said that OU would be a soft place to land after everything I had experienced. In many ways that was true. OU nurtured me, but it was also the place where I challenged and pushed myself further than even I realized I could. I genuinely worked hard there—on myself, on my gymnastics, and on my studies.

For sure, there were so many ways in which the environment was comforting. The coaches at Oklahoma are amazing. They set such a wonderful tone for the athletes. They are like family to us and to each other. In some cases, I mean that literally. K. J. Kindler, the head coach, and Lou Ball, one of two associate head coaches, have been married for years and have two children together. They came to OU in 2006. Tom Haley, who is the other associate head coach, came to OU at the same time as K. J. and Lou. He has three children with his wife, Kelli. Jenn Richardson, OU's Women's Gymnastics trainer, is also a close member of the gym family and has been with

K. J., Lou, and Tom from the start. She has a young daughter as well. They all help each other with their kids and hang out together a lot, even outside of the gym. They genuinely model what it is like to be a close-knit team.

K. J. is the absolute best in the country at what she does. She is a badass in the world of gymnastics—a real powerhouse. If she believes in something, she is not taking no for an answer. She stands up for herself, her team, and her principles. I really look up to her and respect her for that. Women's empowerment is important, and K. J. is a living example of an empowered woman.

In addition to being head coach, K. J. is also the beam coach. She not only does all the choreography for that apparatus, but she does the dance choreography for floor too. After I had been spending time with K. J., people said my beam got so much better. Most of the changes were technical. She made corrections I never had before, and it really just changed my gymnastics. Most of all, it improved my form.

But K. J. is not only a great coach; she is a great person. Despite having a demanding job, she takes the time to cultivate a great relationship with each of the girls on the team. She cares about her athletes in and outside of practice. In the gym, it's always business. She's serious. She knows what her athletes are capable of. But she also cares about what happens in their lives after they leave the gym. From the way she interacts with you, you know she wants what's best for you in school, in life, with boys, with everything. Because her appreciation and concern for people is so genuine, she is great at motivating those around her to be the very best they can be in all ways. She is so intuitive. The minute you walk into the gym, she can tell if you're having a good day or a bad one. She just knows when something is off. She is like a second mom to all the girls—*every single one of us*. As you will see in the pages ahead, she has been such a guiding force for me. There have been so many times when she has pulled me aside to talk, to listen, and to offer a fresh perspective.

Tom and Lou are big presences in the gym too. While Tom was the primary floor coach and Lou was the primary vault coach, they co-coached on bars, so I spent a lot of quality time with each of them. If it was a floor day, I'd go to Tom and do floor; if it was a vault day, I'd go to Lou and do vault, and then Tom and Lou would switch off on bars. They are excellent at what they do, and I always had good times with them, which was great.

Lou is the best collegiate vault coach there is, hands down. He is definitely serious when he needs to be, but he is also a ton of fun. It's that combination that gets such great results. Sometimes, to relieve our stress, he'd turn practice into a game, which always brought the team together. He is such a light in the gym. Lou makes easy conversation and is a truly attentive listener. It's wonderful to have a coach you can really talk to—someone who feels like family. I loved every time I got to go on vault.

Tom and I had a great relationship too. We are similar in a lot of ways, so I always felt like he really got me. In addition to being the best floor coach there is, he is probably one of the most inspirational people I have ever met, just like Mike Hunger was for me. In fact, he's my biggest inspiration and role model to this day. Even though I've ended my gymnastics career, he still helps me to be my very best self. Tom saw my potential on bars and floor—and quite frankly, every event. He always wanted me to take things a step further. He believed I could be perfect every single time. He trusted that I could do all the hard skills and the connections. And on those occasions when I had a step on my dismount after an otherwise perfect routine, he didn't have to say much because he understood I was already aware of my mistake. He would tell me what I needed to know to improve, but more importantly he'd remind me of how good I truly am and how much better I can be. I appreciated the tough love and the pushes as much as the confidence he gave me every day. The other great thing about Tom is that he has nicknames for every single person in the gym. Sometimes he called me Swags; other times he called me Margherita because my full name is Margaret. It was awesome because you'd walk in after a long day of classes, and he'd give you a high five, call out your nickname, and ask how it was going. Welcomes don't get much better than that. Then, once you settled in, he'd remind you of your potential and call on you to be undeniable, not just on that day, but on every single day and at every single competition. He had so many motivational mantras, which we bonded over.

The coaches' records speak for themselves: Collectively, they led OU to their first ever NCAA title in 2014. As of the writing of this book, they've led OU to a total of 5 NCAA Championships, 11 top-three national finishes, 12 straight NCAA Regional Championships, 192 All-American honors, and 12 Big 12 Championships.

The atmosphere at OU was nurturing in other ways too. I actually had a social life for the first time. It was so much better for me than high school. When you're a freshman, you live with the other members of your class in the freshman dorm. My roommate Alex Marks and I were very close with two girls who lived across the hall from us, Jade Degouveia and Brehanna Showers, so we kind of did everything together. Jade and Brehanna were on the gymnastics team with me as well. It was so awesome to have people around who were experiencing a lot of the same adventures as I was. You know, I met some of my absolute best friends that year. We walked to classes together, went to the training room together, and ate at the café in the dorm together.

I loved the training room. That's where all the athletes go to rehab their injuries. It was so cool to meet new people, especially those involved in other sports. I enjoyed hanging out with my new friends after practice and on weekends. I was never able to do that before. It was also nice to go and cheer for them at their games and matches and to have them come and cheer for me too. Nobody in high school really knew much about my gymnastics life until maybe Worlds or Olympic Trials.

I went to football, basketball, soccer, baseball, and volleyball games as often as I could, and because so many of my freshman-year dormmates were on the softball team, I went to their games too.

To be surrounded by so much athletic talent at OU was a gift I never took for granted. During my time at school, former Heisman Trophy winners Baker Mayfield (with the Tampa Bay Buccaneers at the time of writing this), and Kyler Murray (with the Arizona Cardinals) played for OU teams, as did the Atlanta Hawks' Trae Young. And my roommate Nicole Mendes represented Mexico in softball at the 2020 Summer Olympics. These were just a few of the amazingly accomplished people I got to see in action. I tried to soak in as many sports events as I could while I was there, and I always enjoyed watching the televised games with my family when I was home for the holidays.

Because everything was so new to me, it did take a while for me to open up. But once I did, I ended up having so much fun.

Eating at the café was an entirely new experience too. I enjoyed meals again, not only because of my friends' company, but because of the way the coaches believed in nourishing your body. Their mission was to educate us about food and healthy eating. They wanted us to fuel our body so we could achieve optimal performance. They taught us to think about what we were putting into our system, and what each particular food does for us. So, if I picked up a banana, for instance, I was expected to think about why I was eating it. I was expected to know what kind of fuel it was providing. I was expected to be aware that it's a great source of potassium, which regulates fluids, something that's important for you after you sweat a lot. The coaches wanted us to know which foods could help us recover after an intense workout. They wanted us to make eating choices before and after practice that would get us ready for the next day or for the next competition. We were given handouts that explained what kinds of foods could help us maintain energy. Athletes at the Division I level want to be able to do everything they can to be the best at what they do, and fueling the body properly helps with that goal. They taught us how to rebuild muscle that had broken down during our practice sessions, not just by which foods we ate, but by when we ate them. And carbs were definitely welcome at our table. These are all lessons that I have adopted for life because they not only helped me remain strong for practice and competitions, but they helped me keep a clear head when I studied too. Eating was fun and satisfying again.

As much of a good time as I was having during my freshman year, those first weeks were admittedly a little tough. I was no longer having to do half of my schoolwork online and I was definitely excited about that, but there were some technical things that took a while for me to get used to. The computer is your lifeline in college, and I just couldn't seem to master this thing called Canvas, which is where your schedule is listed, and where your class assignments and notes are located. To put it mildly, I had absolutely no clue how to work it. I didn't even know what my login was the first day of class, which was kind of tragic for me. I'm a perfectionist and love knowing how to do everything, but I was totally lost. I felt overwhelmed and had to ask a lot of people for help, which was something I didn't often do. I honestly didn't know if I was going to make it. But thankfully we had advisors, professors, mentors, coaches, and an amazing trainer to show us the way.

I've always had the mindset that each day is a new day; I'm not going to worry about what happened yesterday. I am usually able to set myself forward on my own, but the person at OU who really helped me handle my perfectionism and occasional worries was my trainer Jenn Richardson. From the very beginning, she could read me like a book. She helped me in so many ways. She was someone who could instantly tell if something was off. She would always make herself available to listen and point me in the right direction.

In fact, she did that for everyone. She is the type of person who keeps her eye on all the girls on the team, but especially the freshmen. She knows the transition to college has its challenges. You're away from home and you're doing everything for yourself. I traveled the world before this, but even then, a lot of my arrangements were made for me. I was expected to focus mainly on my gymnastics. When you're at school, everyone has to develop stronger time management skills. Those of us who were involved in athletics had to balance our training and competitions with classes, papers, all the extracurricular activities college life includes, and an active social life too. Jenn always wanted to be sure we weren't being pulled in too many directions. She stressed the importance of being mentally and emotionally healthy as well as physically healthy. Everyone felt as if they could come and talk to her even if it was about things that weren't gymnastics related, such as relationship issues, family issues, or school issues. All those kinds of concerns play a part in your success academically and gymnastically, so she was an outlet for so many people whenever stressors were high. Her door was always open. Besides, we spent so much time with her every day because she was the one giving us rehab and taping us before practice, it was just natural to talk with her. Even though she emphasized being independent and taking care of ourselves, she was the one we went to whenever we were feeling sick or feeling anything at all. Our bond with her was strong throughout our entire college career.

In the same way that adjusting to all the new systems academically was challenging, I found my first gymnastics practices surprisingly tough too. I never expected that. In many ways, my freshman year was a dream come true. I remember it so well. But it really didn't feel that way on my first day in the gym.

It was the beginning of preseason. That's when we had conditioning really early in the morning before classes. It was so different from what I was used to, I had to wrap both my head and my body around the changes. I found myself jokingly thinking again, *Oh my gosh, I don't know if I'm going to make it*. Then later, after going to a full day of classes, we had afternoon practice where we had to do this warm-up called the running warm-up. It's agilities based, so it involves a lot of sprinting and jumping. This was different from my usual warm-up, which was always preceded by weight training. But as with anything new, once you do it a few times, you adapt. Often, it's the change that's more challenging than the task itself.

After a few practices, what I found so interesting was how smart and strategic our assignments and conditioning plans were. In elite training you get thirty-plus hours of training a week, whereas in college, the NCAA limits you to just twenty hours per week so you have enough time for academics. Because we had less time in the gym and fewer reps, the coaches at OU set very high expectations for the time we did have. Everything we did was designed for maximum gain.

A DAY OF PRACTICE AT OU

During the preseason, from August to December, we would meet at 6:00 or 6:30 a.m. for forty-five minutes—no longer and no shorter. During that time, we would do a lot of high-intensity interval training, cycle workouts, track workouts, or swimming. Then we'd head to our classes.

When we returned in the afternoon for practice, which usually ran from 1:00 to 4:15 p.m., we would go directly to our trainer, who taped us up. Then we'd get our heat packs, do stretching and roll outs, and move on to warm-ups, where we either did jump rope, did something we called the running warm-up, or just ran around the floor.

Since we conditioned in the morning, we'd follow warm-ups with three events—either vault, bars, and beam or floor, bars, and beam. We only did one leg event a day to help save our body, our knees, and our ankles. I always thought switching off days like that was a really smart thing to do. We spent the same amount of time at each event.

We would complete our practice by stretching and rolling out. Then, we had to coldtub, which is the process of fully submerging your body in icy water to help decrease inflammation. We would also get a massage after every practice, which was amazing. The massage was typically fifteen minutes long. The therapists would flush out our legs, and if you experienced back pain, they would rub out your back as well. It was an attention to our well-being that we all really appreciated.

Most days, food was catered in, so we didn't have to make dinner on our own. It was a great way to refuel and was viewed as the perfect end to practice.

By the way, when preseason was over, and our season was underway, we no longer did the morning workout. Everything was combined into one long session, which ran from

1:00 to 5:00 p.m. So instead of starting our day with conditioning, we simply followed our warm-ups and our three events with conditioning at the end of practice.

Another big difference I would have to adapt to was the compact nature of the competition season. In elite gymnastics the meets were spread out over the course of the year, but college meets ran between January and April of each year. If your team made it into the finals, fighting for the title meant that you would have competed in thirteen or more meets by the end of that three-month period. I knew it would take some getting used to, but I was ready for the challenge.

I was determined to embrace the newness, confident that it could help me be the best I could be and that it would also ready me and the team to win a National Championship. In the process I think I developed a new level of endurance and strength.

One thing I didn't have a hard time getting used to in college was the emphasis on camaraderie. As I mentioned before, college gymnastics is much more team oriented than elite gymnastics. Every single step of your athletic journey is taken with your teammates in mind; it's not an individual pursuit. Everything you do is for the benefit of the group. I loved that so much. I was so happy competing for my team. I genuinely enjoyed going out there and doing what I did for Oklahoma, my coaches, and my fellow Sooners. I really thrived on that sense of unity.

It didn't take long before I was completely on top of my studies and doing really well in practices and meets. I maintained good grades and was having fun with my gymnastics. I was doing exactly what I set out to do.

But of course, nothing is all sunshine and rainbows the whole time. About halfway into the season, I landed one of my passes just fine, but afterward, the knee I had surgery on during the previous year began to hurt. Apparently, I developed bone chips because I didn't let my knee heal fully before pushing myself to get back into shape for Olympic Trials. Now that choice was coming back to haunt me. It was definitely a bump in the road, but one I would have to take in stride. I took a couple of weeks off just to rest it and had yet another surgery after the season ended.

I still managed to finish the season strong though. We ended up going to Nationals. The individual awards were on the first day of competition, followed by qualifications for the team final. I was favored to win the all-around. We started on floor, which went great. I hit my routine. Vault was pretty good. Bars was great. Then we ended on balance beam, and I actually had a fall on my front tuck. I couldn't believe it. I hadn't had a fall the whole year. I *never* fell on that skill. I was so, so upset, not only because I lost the all-around, but because the fall really took me by surprise. All my perfectionist angst came out again.

Later that evening, K. J. texted me and asked me to meet her. She just wanted to be there for me. She said whatever I needed to do I should do— whether that was to talk it out, cry it out, or hug it out—it would be okay. That's what I meant when I said earlier that she is such a great person. She really got me past that moment so I could move forward and help the team do what we were there to do.

The next day of the competition was going to be the team final, which is the most important. It was what we had been working for all year. We were focused on it throughout preseason, throughout the actual season, throughout it all. So, I did the only thing I could do. I got into a positive mindset. I told myself: *You can't focus on that mistake. You have to turn it around and do what you've done the whole year long. You never fall or make mistakes like that, so just make it right.*

When the team final rolled around, we started on bars. We had a great bar rotation, and we could just feel the energy. It was as if we all knew we were going to win this competition. I've never felt anything like that. We all stuck our bar dismounts, and it was just like the craziest feeling ever. And then I went to beam. I didn't even think about the day before. I wasn't the least bit nervous for that routine this time, and I absolutely nailed it. I got a 10.0 during the team finals, which was crazy because at Nationals, after each of the six judges score your routine, they have to take the average of the totals, then drop the highest and lowest score. I had four 10.0s—enough 10.0s to get a 10.0 in the competition. It was the fourth 10.0 ever scored on that event at the NCAA Championship, and the first earned in team finals. After that happened, the whole team knew that we were going to win the Championships. It was another in a string of absolute dreams come true for me. I cannot explain the joy I felt when I landed the final vault of the whole competition. I was the last one to go, and I stuck it. It was just magical. Everyone was jumping and screaming. I remember sprinting down the runway after that landing. I could hear all the cheering. When I reached my teammates, I hugged every single one of them.

Oh, and did I mention that I was named Big 12 Newcomer of the Year . . . or that I had my first Gym Slam that season too?! A Gym Slam is when you score a perfect 10.0 on each apparatus. I earned a 10.0 on vault on January 21, 2017; a 10.0 on beam on February 3, 2017; a 10.0 on floor one week later on February 10, 2017; and a 10.0 on bars on March 4, 2017.

HOW SCORING IS DONE AT THE DIVISION I COLLEGIATE LEVEL

Calculating an Individual Gymnast's Scores at Collegiate Competitions: If all Special Requirements are met, each routine on bars, beam, and floor starts with a base value of 9.4 and builds to a 10.0 through various skill connections, bonus, and difficulty. On vault, the worth of each skill is determined by its entry style and difficulty of the flight element. For example, as of the writing of this book, a routine including a Yurchenko full would have a start value of 9.95 whereas a routine with a Yurchenko one and a half would have a start value of 10.0.[4] Judges will deduct points from the start value of each routine for flaws or mistakes. Because the judges are looking for as close to a flawless execution of skills as possible, deductions can be as little as a half of a tenth of a point. They catch everything! Once the judges have individually arrived at a score for

4 Clarifications for the upcoming NCAA season are usually released in November prior to the season.

the routine, scores must be flashed at the same time along with the start value they came up with. Again, judges must remain within the allowed score range of each other.

Calculating Team Scores: Six gymnasts from the team are selected beforehand to compete on the four apparatuses. The lowest score among the athletes is dropped; and the top five scores from the team are tallied to arrive at the team's total combined score.

Objectively speaking, my first year was definitely not perfect, but in my mind it was as perfect as any year could be. There was the injury, yes, but coming out on top in the end like that was just so amazing. Going to OU and winning the National Championship with my awesome teammates after not making the Olympics somehow made the whole journey worthwhile.

When I think back on the year, and particularly on wiping my mind clean before going into the team finals at the NCAA Championships, I am reminded of just how important it is to move on and to focus on the things that empower you, because that is how you grow, excel, and succeed.

Something said during the NCAA Championships helped my parents move on from the pain a little bit too. During his coverage of the competition, Bart Conner remarked, "Maggie was second in the world in the all-around in 2015. And yet mysteriously left off the 2016 Olympic team— did not even earn an alternate spot. So she has all the capabilities of every one of those young ladies who came home from Rio with an Olympic gold medal."[5] It was comforting for them, and me, to hear someone of his stature acknowledge what had happened.

* * *

5 *Athlete A.* Directed by Bonni Cohen and Jon Shenk. Netflix, 2020. 1:36:15

In other news, by the summer of my freshman year, Nassar was facing criminal charges in *three* separate courts. The first set of charges, which I mentioned earlier, were heard in *federal* court. There, in July of 2017, he pleaded guilty to three child pornography charges and destruction of evidence. The second set of charges, also mentioned earlier, were heard in *state* court in Ingham County, Michigan, where he faced twenty-six counts of criminal sexual conduct—a fraction of the total complaints the MSU police department would ultimately receive. Nassar subsequently pleaded guilty to seven counts of criminal sexual conduct in the first degree in exchange for prosecutors dropping eight other charges against him and for withholding charges related to many of the other sexual assault claims that arose in the interim. The third set of charges were also heard in *state* court in Eaton County, Michigan, where he faced thirteen additional charges of criminal sexual conduct. He later pleaded guilty to three of those counts in the first degree. As part of Nassar's plea deal in both state courts, he agreed that the court could take into consideration testimony from any complainant during the sentencing hearing.

Over time, Nassar would also face more than two hundred civil lawsuits, including the one I and other survivors filed against him and MSU, USA Gymnastics, and the US Olympic & Paralympic Committee.

It seemed the legal team was having a number of their own wins.

CHAPTER ELEVEN
SOLIDARITY

Unity is strength . . . where there
is teamwork and collaboration,
wonderful things can be achieved.

—MATTIE STEPANEK

Solidarity was the continued theme of my sophomore year. A team has to be in sync to win a national title together, and that's exactly what we did as freshmen. Now that we were sophomores hitting our stride, I could only imagine what other great things were ahead for the Sooners. I was ready for it to be a really great year. Of course, every year has its highs and lows, but I could just tell this one was going to be among my best, and in many ways I was right. I had such high scores the entire season, and just as importantly, I didn't have a severe injury.

My knee was still bothering me, though, so we decided to keep an eye on it in the gym, which was a huge development for me. I wasn't used to that at all. Unlike the philosophy at USA Gymnastics, the OU coaches and our trainer Jenn Richardson believe that if something is hurting you, you should rehab it. You're not going to do as many numbers in practice. You're not going to do the skill that's aggravating it. You're going to sit out that day. Whatever it is that's the problem, whether it's your knee or something else, you're going to let it calm down. That was the rule. By contrast, if something is hurting you when you're an elite gymnast, you work through it. You're not resting it. You're finishing that practice. OU's approach was so markedly different, it definitely helped me get stronger and become a better gymnast.

That wasn't the only thing that made sophomore year so good. It was the year I scored a lot more perfect tens. I had my second Gym Slam! Only two women in NCAA gymnastic history have had two Gym Slams as of the writing of this book. Sophomore year was also when the Sooners followed our prior year's Big 12 Championship win with another Big 12 win. Another happy moment was when I was named Big 12 Gymnast of the Year.

Going into Nationals, we were favored to win again. We were pretty much number one all year. The first day was the individual competition, followed by the qualification for team final. After qualifying with the highest score, we were pumped up and ready to go the next day. I ended up winning the all-around that year, so that was really exciting for me. But more than anything, I was looking forward to competing in the team final. All the girls had grown so close and worked so hard, I wanted a win for every one of us. I wasn't really stuck on winning the all-around. Yes, it felt great to have that achievement, but my ultimate objective was to help the team take home the National Championship trophy.

I'm sad to say that despite our best efforts, we came up short on that goal. We lost by less than one tenth of a point, a deduction that could have been for something as minimal as a flexed big toe. I just remember being so devastated. The whole team was. We were so hard on ourselves because we knew we could have won that—we *should* have won that. My roommate Bre and I couldn't let it go at first. We were so upset. I can't tell you how many times we wished out loud that we could have redone that day, but that's not how competition goes. Right after that, she and I made a pact. We were going to spend the whole summer getting so much better. We were never going to feel that way ever again. Coming up a bit short like that is one of the most frustrating feelings. We worked so hard that whole season. I know every other team did as well, but it was just so disappointing to lose when we were that close. Those feelings only made us want to come back stronger the next year.

Speaking of coming back stronger, survivors of Larry Nassar's abuse were finally going to have our day in court. On December 7, 2017, Nassar was sentenced to sixty years in federal prison on the child pornography charges. But that wasn't the final word on his jail time, because roughly six weeks after that, on January 16, 2018, the seven-day hearing in Ingham County, Michigan began.

So many of us survivors were anticipating this hearing. Detective Sergeant Andrea Munford and Assistant Attorney General Angela Povilaitis wanted to see Nassar pay for his crimes, but they also wanted to help the survivors heal. They knew that giving us a chance to confront our abuser would go a long way toward shifting the power imbalance we felt as young people at the hands of this widely respected doctor who was secretly molesting us. They believed that making a victim-impact statement and using our voices would give us back some control. I am grateful to Andrea, Angela, and Judge Rosemarie Aquilina for respecting our First Amendment rights and making this happen.

However, weeks before this, as preparations for the hearing were under-way, I had to make an important decision. Up until this point, I had been identified as Athlete A to protect my privacy. I didn't yet know how many other survivors might come forward to address Nassar. I had to decide if identifying myself publicly would serve a larger good.

I remember that as a very difficult time. Jenn and K. J. really helped me through that period. One day K. J. and I had breakfast together. That's when I opened up and told her everything that had happened to me. I also told her about the choice I had to make. Together we weighed the pros and cons of the situation. She didn't express an opinion either way. She just wanted me to do what was right for me. She listened to everything I said, knowing it was important for me to have someone I could talk to about my fears, hopes, and expectations, especially because I didn't have my parents there with me in Oklahoma. When I told Jenn, she too made it clear that she supported me in whatever decision I made. K. J. and Jenn played a huge part in helping me get clarity on the subject, and I am very grateful for that.

While I am a deeply private person, I knew that if I came out and said that I was Athlete A, I could help other people in similar situations find the courage to come forward and seek justice too. Helping just one other person would make everything worth it. I just wanted people in similar positions to know they're not alone. I knew that so many other people—men and women, boys and girls—were struggling with this kind of thing. If I could help them by example, if I could say something that made them feel comforted or more empowered, if I could lend a listening ear or be someone they could lean on, then coming out would be worth the trade-off of my privacy. In my heart I knew it was the best thing for me to do.

Once I made up my mind, I had to bring my teammates together to tell them that I was coming forward. I didn't want them to hear or read about it in the news. I wanted to be sure they heard it directly from me. I knew they might need to process the information and that K. J. and Jenn could help them with that. As it turned out, I asked K. J. to tell everybody because I just couldn't do it when the time came. It was such an emotionally charged subject.

I didn't know how my teammates would respond. I knew the people I was closest with would be there for me if I ever needed them, but it was nice to see others on the team reach out and offer their support too. In the end, I felt comfortable that they knew because we were all like sisters. We had gone through other ups and downs together.

It also gave me some peace to know that the school administration had my back as well. Joseph Castiglione, the university's athletic director, was very concerned about my well-being and worked with K. J. and our information director, Lindsey Morrison, to be sure the media respected my space after the news came out.

The next day, on January 9, 2018, I issued the following press release:

STATEMENT FROM MAGGIE NICHOLS

Recently, three of my friends and former National Team members who medaled at the 2012 Olympics have bravely stepped forward to proclaim they were sexually assaulted by USA Gymnastics Team Physician Dr. Larry Nassar.

Today I join them.

I am making the decision to tell my traumatic story and hope to join the forces with my friends and teammates to bring about true change.

Up until now, I was identified as Athlete A by USA Gymnastics, the US Olympic Committee, and Michigan State University. I want everyone to know that he did not do this to Athlete A, he did it to Maggie Nichols.

In the summer of 2015, my coach and I reported this abuse to USA Gymnastics leadership.

I first started [g]ymnastics when I was [3] and since I was a child, I always had the dream of competing for my country in the Olympic Games. I made elite level gymnastics when I was 13. By the time I was 14, I made the USA National Team. I traveled internationally for 4 years attending competitions and in 2015 competed at the World Championships representing our country.

People who watch gymnastics see young girls fly through the air and do all kinds of amazing things. You can imagine that having a good doctor is absolutely necessary to compete at the highest level.

Dr. Larry Nassar was regarded throughout the sport as the very best by coaches and staff throughout the gymnastics community. He was a doctor at Michigan State University and the Olympic and Team USA doctor assigned to us by USA Gymnastics at the Olympic Training Center at the Karolyi Ranch. He was supposed to care for us and treat our injuries. The first time I met Dr. Nassar I was about 13 or 14 years old and receiving treatment for an elbow injury. At the time it seemed like he knew exactly what therapy was necessary for me to recover. Initially, he did nothing unusual.

But when I was 15, I started to have back problems while at a National Team Camp at the Karolyi Ranch. This is when the changes in his medical treatments occurred. My back was really hurting me, I couldn't even really bend down, and I remember he took me into the training room, closed the door and closed the blinds. At the time I thought this was kind of weird but figured it must be okay. I thought he probably didn't want to distract the other girls and I trusted him.

I trusted what he was doing at first, but then he started touching me in places I really didn't think he should. He didn't have gloves on and he didn't tell me what he was doing. There was no one else in the room and I accepted what he was doing because I was told by adults that he was the best doctor and he could help relieve my pain.

He did this "treatment" on me, on numerous occasions.

Not only was Larry Nassar my doctor, I thought he was my friend. He contacted me on Facebook complimenting me and telling me how beautiful I looked on numerous occasions. But I was only 15 and I just thought he was trying to be nice to me. Now I believe this was part of the grooming process I recently learned about.

One day at practice, I was talking to my teammate, and brought up Dr. Nassar and his treatments. When I was talking to her, my coach overheard. I had never told my coach about these treatments. After hearing our conversation, she asked me more questions about it and said it doesn't seem right. I showed her the Facebook messages and told her about what Nassar was doing. My coach thought it was wrong, so she did the right thing and reported this abuse to the USA Gymnastics staff.

USA Gymnastics and the USOC did not provide a safe environment for me and my teammates to train. We were subjected to Dr. Nassar at every National Team Camp[,] which occurred monthly at the Karolyi Ranch. His job was to care for our health and treat our injuries. Instead, he violated our innocence.

I later found out that Michigan State University had ignored complaints against Larry Nassar from other girls going back 20 years and had investigated him for sexual assault in 2014. They never told USA Gymnastics. If they had, I might never have met Larry Nassar and I would never have been abused by him.

I have come to the realization that my voice can have influence over the manner in which our USA athletes are treated.

Throughout everything that has happened, my faith in God has sustained me.

I would like to let everyone know that I am doing OK. My strong faith has helped me endure. It is a work in progress. I will strive to ensure the safety of young athletes who have big dreams just like mine and I will encourage them to stand up and speak if something doesn't seem right.

I want to thank everyone from the bottom of my heart that has helped me through this difficult time. My parents, coaches, and friends who have known about it, and that have stood by my side through it all. I would not have been able to be so strong without each of you.

For several days beginning on January 16, 2018, 156 women reclaimed their power, giving moving victim-impact statements at that hearing. And in many ways, they helped reclaim the power of others who couldn't be there in person. The world watched as they took back their agency one by one. Because the hearing was live streamed, I was able to watch as my mother read a statement in my place. I didn't know if I would be able to read my statement myself.

Again, it was such an emotional situation. I was at school and was the only survivor who was still actively competing in gymnastics at the time, so I am so thankful my mother could use her voice to spread my story further and to make Larry hear my truth. I also think that people don't know how much whole families have been affected by what Larry did, so my mom's presence carried that weight too. I remember so many people reaching out to me afterward to tell me they thought my mom was such a badass. She is so strong. To see her stand up in a difficult moment like that was very inspiring.

Although I wasn't present in the courtroom that day, I did feel heard and relieved after I made my statement to the press days before and my mother read it again in court in my absence.

When the Ingham County, Michigan, hearing ended later that month, Nassar was sentenced to 40 to 174 years in prison.

But the law wasn't done with him yet. Soon after that, the Eaton County, Michigan, hearing began. Sixty-five more women gave impact statements there, and Nassar was sentenced with 40 to 125 years in prison to be served concurrently with the Ingham County sentence, but after the child pornography sentence of sixty years was carried out.

It's safe to say that Larry Nassar will be incarcerated for several lifetimes.

Inspired by the courage displayed during those hearings, more victims came forward in the months to follow.

By May of 2018, Nassar's employer MSU settled with 332 of his victims, myself included, for $500 million. Because the university had looked the other way when allegations surfaced before—some of which dated back to 1997—he had been free to commit crimes at USA Gymnastics. The settlement recognized their culpability. Of that sum, $425 million was to be paid to claimants who had already come forward, and $75 million was to be set aside in a trust to protect future claimants alleging sexual abuse by Nassar.

That season, after a meet between OU and UCLA held in UCLA's Pauley Pavilion, I was honored alongside some of the other outspoken survivors of sexual abuse, including UCLA Bruins volunteer coach and Olympic Gold medalist Jordyn Wieber and former UCLA Bruins gymnasts Jeanette Antolin, Mattie Larson, and Jamie Dantzscher, the latter of whom is also an Olympic medalist. I know the evening was special for Madison Kocian and Kyla Ross too. Both were present, but neither had come out publicly yet. It was a very moving night, during which a video entitled *Together We Rise* was shown in tribute. We stood in a circle at the center of the floor and held hands. The crowd cheered us with teal pom-poms, and we all wore teal ribbons in solidarity. OU and UCLA were rivals that year, so it was great that they made the evening about more than just competition. It was so important for us to put that rivalry aside and come together in unity to support one another and to address a subject that deserves our combined attention and efforts.

I stayed for more than an hour afterward speaking with and signing autographs for young girls. It is so important to me that I bring these issues out in the open and help improve all our safety. Being a role model for young athletes and young people everywhere is a responsibility I take very seriously. I wanted to demonstrate that I had resiliency. That I was continuing to compete and perform at my highest level. That our worst experiences don't define us. That what we do beyond them does. I read somewhere that there are no special prizes for those who had it the hardest, only for those who persevere and overcome their hardships. I wanted to be clear that I had moved on and that I was still striving to be the best in every way. That night really meant so much to me for all those reasons, and I know it meant a lot for my fellow honorees too.

To say this was an eventful year would be an incredible understatement.

CHAPTER TWELVE
SUPPORT

We rise by lifting others.

—ROBERT INGERSOLL

I have always believed in being there for other people, especially for team-mates and those who have been there for me. My junior year called on me and every member of the Sooners to be a support for Jenn Richardson and her husband, Dave. Jenn is someone who has shown up for our entire team whenever we needed her; now it was time for us to show up for her and her family. Dave had been battling with cancer for three years, and it was getting worse. For so many of us on campus in Norman, Oklahoma, far away from our own parents, Dave was a father figure. We would all refer to him as our Norman dad.

Because Jenn was always at the gym, Dave was too, and he'd often bring their young daughter Joie with him. Before he became ill, Dave came to all our meets. He would do anything for us girls on the team. He made such an impact on our lives. In addition to being a police officer, he was a high school football coach, so he was a naturally motivating presence. It hurt us to see him so ill and to see Jenn suffering too. In so many ways, they became a huge part of our 2019 year.

Throughout preseason, we all knew that Dave wasn't doing well, so when the season started, we kind of shifted our focus to something bigger than us. We decided we weren't doing this season for ourselves; we were doing it for him. Our hashtag for the year became #DIFD, meaning *Do It for Dave*. We wore patches with it on our warm-up jackets and wrote it on our hands for every competition.

Although we were trying our best, it wasn't exactly a year of sunshine and rainbows for the team either. We had a lot of injuries, but we worked through them because we had a larger purpose.

I had been having a great season when out of nowhere I had an injury too. I ruptured my plantar fascia at a competition. That's the tissue that connects your heel to the base of your toes. When I took off from my double pike on floor, I felt this big explosion in the sole of my right foot. I knew that it was torn instantly because my heel had been hurting for months before that. I could barely walk on hard ground, so I was honestly kind of relieved when the injury forced me to deal with it properly. I still finished my routine, then I took off for about two weeks, doing just bars at meets until it was better. I got back into the all-around later in the season.

Everyone else worked hard at mending or managing their injuries too. We made it to Big 12s and won, which was great because Regionals qualify to Nationals. This thing we were going through as a team pushed us through every challenge and helped us to stay on top. We always had that mantra in our minds, you know, *Do It for Dave*.

Sometime during midseason, we all went to the hospital to see him before a competition. We knew it was one of his last days. It was so hard. Dave was only forty-five years old and such a good person. I have the picture we took during that visit. We knew he was at the end of life, but we just wanted to see him one more time. He gave us a little speech, and closed by saying, "You guys are going to win this National Championship." We were all crying and had shivers. There was no stopping us now. We knew that we were going to win it too, and that we were going to do it for him. We were determined to fulfill that pledge.

The first day of competition went really well. I stuck my vault, which was good, and then I went to bars and had a great routine. My beam routine went very well too. Next up was floor. I believe it was my first time competing on floor since I ruptured my plantar fascia. At that point, I didn't know what score I needed to win the all-around. All I knew was that I was happy to be in it and I was going to give it everything I had. It turns out, I needed a 9.9 to win and I ended up getting a 9.9250. Because I wasn't aware of what it would take to clinch the all-around, I didn't realize at first that I had won. That's when K. J. came running over to me and was shouting, "You just won. You won the all-around!" I was ecstatic. It was just so super exciting. I was so happy. Then Holly Rowe came over and interviewed me on TV. It was such an awesome feeling. But again, my goal was to help the team win the National Championship and to do it for Dave. So right away I turned my shift around. I mean, it was really cool that I did back-to-back all-arounds, but after that, I had to change my focus. The goal was for the *team* to win. We were going to do it. I just knew in my gut we had it in us.

So, we started on bars. We had a good bar rotation. I wouldn't say it was great. But you could feel that the momentum was there—not all the way there, but close. Then we went to beam, and we had an outstanding beam rotation. Like it was out of this world, it was so good. After that I think we all knew the win was ours. We were going to do this. Next was floor, and we had an okay floor rotation. Then one girl in the lineup had a fall and we all knew we had to nail our routines. The three or four girls who went next did just that. Every one of them nailed it. That got us thinking, *Okay, this is ours. We're going to clinch this.* Thankfully, we had a great rotation. We all made our vaults. I just remember waiting with bated breath as Brenna Dowell, who was anchoring, stuck her vault cold. Everyone was jumping up in the air after that, screaming and crying. The atmosphere was electric. The feeling was unreal. We were all so excited. We did what we set out to do. You know, we all did it for him. That's who we did it for. It was all for Dave. At the end of our emotional hospital visit with Dave weeks earlier, he said that we were going to win this championship, and then we did. He passed away shortly after that visit, but we have so many pictures of us pointing up to the sky the day we won because we were sure he was watching over us. We just knew that he was there the whole time. That mantra, *Do It for Dave*, carried us. That was probably the best moment of my entire career. It was so amazing.

Jenn had taken some time off and then came back a couple of meets before Nationals, so having her there that day was just so special. And the craziest thing happened. There's always this big debate about what song the team is going to play, and this time K. J. picked "24K Magic," by Bruno Mars. Dave's favorite song.

Sometimes gymnastics has a way of reminding us that some things in life are bigger than the sport. This was another one of those times for me.

CHAPTER THIRTEEN
GRATITUDE

Approach today with gratitude,
understanding, openness,
knowing that it offers
potential & possibilities.
Knowing that every moment is an
opportunity to reflect, reset, and
move forward with intention.

—@SUSTAINABLEBLISSCO

I returned to school the next year as a senior. Going into preseason, the Sooners were ranked number one. In the beginning of the actual season, everything was still going according to plan. I was competing really well. My knee was doing all right. Nothing too crazy was happening. By the time the season was underway, we were still ranked number one. Then in February we started hearing rumblings about the coronavirus. We weren't sure what it meant for us, so the season continued as usual.

We even had our senior night on March 6, which usually takes place after our last home meet at Norman. We competed against Michigan that evening. On this special occasion, it's traditional for seniors to pick the leo we'll wear. We chose a simple crimson one with white sleeves and jewels all over the front.

As busy as K. J. is, she always takes the time to do extra thoughtful things on that night. She decorated our lockers with pictures from our four years on the team, and she put up quotes she selected for each of us, which was so nice. She even filled the room with balloons. She really went the extra mile to express her love for us.

It's also traditional for K. J. to give a speech about each of us at the end of the meet. She typically talks about our accolades, but more importantly, she talks about who we are as people. It's always a special night, made all the more special this time by the fact that it was Jade Degouveia's, Brehanna Showers's, and my turn to be celebrated. It was bittersweet too because it was going to be the last time we three would compete in the Lloyd Noble Center (aka the LNC), the arena in Norman where our home meets are held.

That night, we started on vault, and I actually got a 10.0. It was my twenty-second career perfect 10. Then we went to bars, and I got a 9.95. I had a really good routine. I got a 9.95 on beam, and a 9.95 on floor as well. After my floor routine was completed, I was waiting for everybody else to finish. I was just taking in the moment. When the competition ended, K. J. recognized each of us in a way only she could.

She opened by talking about the power of three. She explained how an atom cannot exist without a proton, a neutron, and an electron; how three primary colors—red, yellow, and blue—alone make all the colors of the rainbow; and how the triangle is the strongest geometrical shape, made of three sides and three corners. Then she went on to say that Jade, Bre, and I exemplify the power of three. And it's true, we were always strongest as a team—as a family.

She spoke about Jade first, then Bre, and in both instances she nailed the best attributes of these great athletes and friends.

When K. J. got to me, her words were a reminder of just how far I had come since freshman year and how many people—near and far—supported and cheered me on through it all. She said,

Maggie entered OU quietly. She kept to herself. She worked through practice each day with determination and a low-key presence. And now, she will depart OU loudly, and having made epic impacts on the University of Oklahoma, NCAA Gymnastics, and the entire gymnastics community worldwide.

I recall her freshman season, 2017, vividly. I was a bit naive and underestimated her popularity nationally. We traveled to West Virginia for our first away competition of the year, and they had a record crowd. There were families that had traveled hours just to get a glimpse of her competing. After the competition she was swarmed with admirers waiting (some patiently, some impatiently) for her autograph, a picture, or a glance their way. We (me) were unprepared for this response . . . Fast forward one hour later and the lines and people continued. When we had to cut off the autographs to get back to the hotel, I remember a man yelling, "We traveled 5 hours just to meet her." That is when I recognized we had just witnessed the "Maggie Nichols effect."

After sharing aspects of my record, K. J. continued. She knew firsthand how much my work to help other survivors and all people struggling with challenges in their life means to me.

Maggie is recognized as a force on social media with a following that looks forward to her posts on positivity and life insights daily. She strives to inspire others and have a global impact. She recognizes her parents as her biggest influence in life and is thankful for all the sacrifices they have made.

During her sophomore year, Maggie changed the gymnastics world when she bravely opened up, publicly identifying herself as Athlete "A."

We are all a sum of our experiences and her courage to have a voice when staying silent could have been easier and more comfortable was the epitome of tough. She was met with praise, and her iconic decision has opened the door for the many other women who would find their voices.

It was a very moving night. After all the reminiscing, praise, and out-pouring of emotion, Jade, Bre, and I were more than ready to dominate our last season of collegiate gymnastics.

In just a week, we were expecting to have a competition in Minnesota. It's my home state, so I was very excited because family and friends were coming to watch. The arena was sold out. One of my coaches from TCT, Rich Stenger, was telling me that everyone was looking forward to it. It was just going to be this super amazing competition.

As a senior, I knew that it might be the last time a lot of people could see me compete live. But two days before we were set to travel there, the venue announced that they weren't going to let the public come into the arena due to what they were now calling Covid-19. I was devastated. It felt so much like that time my family and friends gathered in Minnesota for my first com-petition as an elite gymnast and I hurt my knee. (Remember that?) But at least the meet was still going to be in Minnesota. That was some consolation.

We went to practice that day. Training proceeded as usual. But the very next day, K. J. texted the seniors and told us that plans had changed again. We weren't going after all. The meet was canceled.

We still went to practice, unsure of what else to do. But halfway through training, K. J. announced a meeting in the team room. That's when she told us the news that the entire season was done. The whole campus was being sent home. The place was being shut down.

Everyone was shocked, but the seniors on the team—Bre, Jade, and I—were just absolutely gutted. We still had so much left to show everyone. We felt that this was going to be a season for the records.

Bre asked what we should do. We were so sad because our careers were over in the blink of an eye. It was completely out of the blue, in the middle of the season. We didn't get to finish. I was vying for my third-straight NCAA all-around title, and Bre, Jade, and I were going for our third NCAA team National Championship.

I know so many of you reading this book are recalling how your own lives were disrupted during this time too. It took the whole world by surprise, not just us. We all felt it in our own way.

The next day, we met as a team at the stadium where the academic center is located. Jade, Bre, and I wrote our farewells, thanking Sooner Nation for everything they had done for us. We were still so upset. Although K. J. told everyone we were free to leave and that we should make whatever plans we had to in order to get home, those of us who were seniors needed a beat to process what happened. We knew on some level the school made the right decision. The important thing was to keep everyone as safe as possible and not jeopardize anyone's life or health, but it was still hard.

Bre, Jade, and I actually ended up taking a trip together. We went to Orange Beach in Alabama and lay in the sun for a couple of days. It coincided with spring break, so we didn't have any Zoom classes yet. We took that moment to let it sink in that we were done with gym. It was over. We were not going back to practice anymore.

While hanging out together, I decided to write a statement to the NCAA, telling them we believed we deserved another year of eligibility because we didn't get to finish out the season or make it to the Championships. The post got a lot of retweets and likes from influential people like Lincoln Riley, Oklahoma's former head football coach. Clearly his players were struggling with the same issues we were.

Over time, a couple of things helped to ease my mind. The first was a sense of gratitude. I had such an amazing collegiate career. I am recognized as the best all-around gymnast in the history of the NCAA because I have the greatest number of scores 39.9 and above. I was one of only twelve gymnasts to ever complete the Gym Slam, and the first in NCAA history to do it twice (in 2017 and 2018). I was a seventeen-time All–Big 12 selection and a two-time Big 12 Gymnast of the Year. I earned six NCAA individual championships. Additionally, I earned All-America honors thirty times. I helped lead the Sooners to a 111–2 overall record and three undefeated seasons that included winning three Big 12 titles and a pair of all-around National Championships in 2018 and 2019. I was also presented with the Arthur Ashe Courage Award at the 2018 ESPYs and won the 2019 Honda Sport Award, given annually to the student athlete who is considered the best in collegiate athletics.

I was comforted too by what our coaches told us. Since we were number one as a team at the time our season was suspended, we were in fact the season champions. Bre and I remained in Norman for a couple of months after that, finishing out the school year off campus. In retrospect, I was glad that we were able to have senior night before everything shut down. That was some form of closure and celebration for us. I valued that experience even more because of the circumstances that followed.

I also appreciated the moniker Simone Biles gave me during my time at OU, a nickname that resurfaced in the press around the time of our senior season's premature end. She called me *the Michael Jordan of collegiate gymnastics*. I think the name came from the fact that I was a comfort for a lot of the other girls on my team. My consistency was an important factor in our team spirit. The level of gymnastics I was competing at was apparent in the number of 10.0s I had achieved too. I also think the name had something to do with the number of injuries I had and was able to rebound from. After all, I'd had four knee surgeries by then.

Of course, I couldn't resist having a little fun with the compliment. I posed for a picture wearing all my rings the way Michael Jordan once did, then I posted his picture and mine side by side on social media. I never let the nickname put too much pressure on me though. I just thought it was cool to be called that and to have the respect of a former teammate whom I respect too.

When I accepted that my career as a gymnast was over, I had to do what I always did: look forward to the future. Even though I arrived at OU truly disappointed that I didn't make the Olympic team, I focused on being and doing the best I possibly could, and because of that positive attitude I accomplished so much. Ironically, despite not making the Olympic team, I beat every former Olympian I ever competed against at the college level. This naturally affirmed that I can never let my circumstances limit my prospects for greatness. It was time to heed that important lesson and turn around my thinking about Covid's impact on my senior year.

K. J., Lou, and Tom had scheduled team meetings for us on Zoom a couple times a week and graciously included us seniors. We would just talk and do activities. The meetings were really more like check-ins to make sure we were doing all right. That was a big help during our transition. The coaches also sent out guidelines for voluntary conditioning. They wanted to keep us motivated. In a way I still felt like a part of the team even though I knew I wouldn't be competing anymore.

In fact, I was still hoping to be part of the team in a different role once in-person classes and training resumed. I had spoken with K. J. sometime earlier about becoming the student volunteer coach in my fifth year while I pursued my master's degree. She had agreed, so if this pause due to Covid didn't take too long, I kind of knew that was going to be my next step in gymnastics.

Once the summer arrived, I tried to stay as active as possible. I went on super long walks. I made up conditioning circuits of my own because I loved working out. I really enjoyed that aspect of taking charge of my own development. The pandemic proved to me that just because you're not on a team doesn't mean you can't still challenge yourself.

Throughout my elite and college careers, whenever I was going through a difficult time or had an injury that was hard to come back from, I would tell myself, *this isn't happening **to** you; it's happening **for** you.* I would also follow up by asking myself, *What is this going to grow you into? What is this going to teach you?* The same thinking applied to the challenges I faced during the pandemic. I had to ask myself, *What is the end to your career as a gymnast* *and the beginning of your time as a student assistant coach all about? What are you going to do with this opportunity?*

My answer was clear: I was going to use all my experience to help these girls be the best they could be. I had a wonderful volunteer assistant coach from my sophomore through senior years named Ashley Kerr. Now I was going to be joining her in that role. Ashley was a huge part of my success when I was competing and an invaluable asset to the team overall. The special touch she brought to the gym contributed so much to how well we performed. I was going to watch and learn from her. I was also going to follow the examples of K. J., Lou, and Tom, and every other great coach I ever had.

K. J., for instance, coaches everyone differently. She knows how each girl is going to absorb criticism. So, I set out to know every single athlete on the team too. I wanted to know who they were as people. I observed what motivated them and how they responded to difficulties. I was also going to use all my experience as a recent gymnast to visualize the corrections they needed to make. I wanted my input to land as constructively as possible and to stick. And I was going to be sensitive to the fact that some of the girls experienced a gap in their collegiate career due to the pandemic. Even though they were offered an extra year of eligibility, that gap had still been somewhat disruptive to their training and conditioning. Given all I had experienced in life, I think I knew a little about modeling how to come back from adversity. So those were the things I set out to do.

During those two years as a student assistant coach, it felt so good whenever the girls came up to me and said, "You helped me so much," or when they would text me to ask, "Are you going to be at practice today? I need you here." I genuinely believe I brought a sense of comfort to the girls on the team. They relied on me in a lot of ways, and it was rewarding to know they trusted and respected me. I loved that they wanted me at their practices and meets. I really felt as if I made a difference.

They impacted me too. I had such good relationships with most of the girls because I was on the team with them before. Knowing them for that long allowed me to see how far they had come and how much they accomplished over time. I had seen them through each step of the way. Every little thing, especially during our final season, was so rewarding to me—the competitions, the successes, but also the relationships that I built and the lives I influenced.

And seeing the Sooners take the NCAA championship again in 2022 was pretty awesome as well.

Outside of school and coaching, I was still committed to helping other gymnasts and athletes find the courage to come forward and share their stories of sexual abuse or other types of abuse in their respective sports. In the summer of 2020, just before beginning my master's program, Netflix released a documentary film called *Athlete A*. As the title suggests, my story features prominently alongside Rachael Denhollander's, Jamie Dantzscher's, and Jessica Howard's.

It was important for me and my parents to participate and provide details of the story the public was less aware of. Before this movie, few people knew the extent of the horrible things that had happened behind the scenes, or USA Gymnastics' role in it. Everyone knew about Larry Nassar, but the film exposes some of his enablers too, and the toxic environment that had existed for years at the national camp and in USA Gymnastics gyms across the country.

The film also celebrates the journalists at the *IndyStar*, and their editor, Steve Berta, who dug deep to bring the truth to light. Nobody could have imagined a local newspaper breaking such a big and important international story, but their work proves our need for investigative reporting with ties to and a deeper caring for our communities. I admire everyone involved at the paper for their persistence and their sense of justice. I have such gratitude for what they did—and appreciation for the work of the film's directors, Bonni Cohen and Jon Shenk, too. The documentary, in many ways, got me thinking about writing this book, as there was still so much more for me to reflect on and say. I hope you view the film and this memoir as strong companion pieces. Together I think they reveal the good side of this story as well as the bad. There were many people besides Nassar who abandoned their civic duty and the girls and young women of gymnastics, but I think both pieces also acknowledge the many people who stood up and helped restore our sense of dignity and justice. Because I am generally an optimistic person, most days I choose to focus on the latter group of people.

I must also add that when *Athlete A* was released, USA Gymnastics' current CEO, Li Li Leung, released a public statement as follows:

> *We are deeply committed to learning from the mistakes of the past and the mishandling of the horrific abuse perpetrated by Larry Nassar. In order to do that, we must listen with open hearts to Maggie Nichols' story, and the experiences of other survivors, so that we can truly understand the impact it had, and the circumstances that led to it and enabled it for too long.*

> *Because of the bravery of Maggie and other survivors who have come forward, there have been transformational reforms across the sport. Within USA Gymnastics, under an entirely new leadership team, we have implemented stronger policies and preventative measures, launched multiple educational efforts, and made sweeping organizational, leadership[,] and personnel changes. Most importantly, we have prioritized changing the sub-culture within our community that allowed this to happen. We owe these survivors an incredible debt of gratitude for igniting these changes across the sport.*

> *Despite these changes, we recognize that the work is not yet done. We must keep listening, keep evolving[,] and keep improving—and we are committed to doing so.*

It looks like the organization is taking steps in the right direction, though they still have a long way to go.

CHAPTER FOURTEEN
SACRIFICE

Strength is the product of struggle.
You must do what others don't to
achieve what others won't.

—HENRY ROLLINS

A s you know by now, goal setting has served me very well in life. When I decided to get my master's degree in education and intercollegiate administration, I was not only committed to balancing my student assistant coaching responsibilities with my studies, I promised myself I would strive for a 4.0 GPA. As with all the big objectives I set for myself, I knew there might be some sacrifices. Sleep was one of them. But I am happy to say that on May 14, 2022, I graduated with that goal fulfilled. It's been great to be at Oklahoma for six years—four as an undergraduate and two as a graduate student. Overall, it's been such an amazing experience, and getting my master's in a field I am passionate about is icing on the cake. It is also a milestone that reminds me of how far I have come.

There was another very important goal to me that was fulfilled during the time I was in graduate school. Other survivors of the Larry Nassar ordeal and I set out earlier to hold his enablers accountable for their part in what had happened to us. In many ways, Nassar didn't commit his crimes alone. There were plenty of people and organizations that shirked their responsibility to stop him. First, as you will recall, we sued and settled with MSU for $500 million to be distributed among hundreds of his victims. Then, in December of 2021, after a long five-year battle, we finally agreed to a $380 million settlement with USA Gymnastics and the United States Olympic & Paralympic Committee. In addition to the monetary terms, the latter settlement also required victims of abuse to hold positions within USA Gymnastics in a move intended to strengthen athlete protections. While the entire board of USA Gymnastics had been replaced earlier, this was an additional way to ensure that people with the girls' best interests would always be involved in the decision-making. This was a crucial piece of the settlement in my mind.

But while this was another vital step in making things right and safer in the world of gymnastics, several of us were still not satisfied with the way the FBI had handled our allegations. We believed their inaction continued to put girls and young women at risk well after Nassar's earlier victims came forward. In July of 2019, the Office of the Inspector General published a report detailing all the stunning ways in which the FBI had failed us. The OIG, as the office is called, is responsible for government oversight, meaning it investigates wrongdoing within government agencies.

By September of 2021, it was time for us to voice our concerns at a US Senate Judiciary Committee hearing. Simone Biles, McKayla Maroney, Aly Raisman, and I testified. It was an emotional and exhausting day as we relived our traumas before the committee and the public. The goal was to ask the committee to hold accountable the individuals at the FBI who had been so careless with our truth and our safety. After addressing MSU's and USA Gymnastics' and the Olympic & Paralympic Committee's accountability, it was now the FBI's turn, because unlike the other organizations that had let us down, members of the FBI are sworn to protect us. We had to know why they mismanaged the investigation, disregarded our rights, and put so many additional girls in harm's way. And why their inaction was continuing. Why were there no repercussions for those who behaved negligently since the OIG report was released?

The senators at the hearing had read the report, but you probably haven't. So let me include Inspector General Michael Horowitz's own summary of the findings from a portion of his statement before the committee that day. I highlighted key parts for you and added some of my own comments and clarifications in the margins.

FACTUAL FINDINGS OF THE OIG REPORT

USA GYMNASTICS REPORTS SEXUAL ASSAULT ALLEGATIONS TO THE FBI'S INDIANAPOLIS FIELD OFFICE IN JULY 2015; INDIANAPOLIS'S INVESTIGATIVE RESPONSE.

In July 2015, following a USA Gymnastics internal investigation into allegations of sexual assault by Nassar against multiple gymnasts, USA Gymnastics President and Chief Executive Officer Stephen D. Penny, Jr., reported the allegations to the FBI's Indianapolis Field Office. During the meeting, among other things, Penny described graphic information that three gymnasts (Gymnasts 1, 2, and 3), all of whom were minors at the time of the alleged sexual assaults, had provided to USA Gymnastics. Penny further informed the FBI that the three athletes were available to be interviewed. Penny noted during the meeting that Nassar told USA Gymnastics that he was performing a legitimate medical procedure during his treatments of the gymnasts and denied sexually assaulting them. Further, Penny provided the FBI with a thumb drive containing PowerPoint slides and videos that Nassar had provided to USA Gymnastics of Nassar performing his purported medical technique on athletes.

Shortly after the meeting, USA Gymnastics advised Nassar that he should no longer attend USA Gymnastics events, and Nassar retired from his USA Gymnastics position in September 2015. However, Nassar continued to maintain his positions at MSU, Twistars USA Gymnastics Club, and Holt High School.

Over the next 6 weeks, the Indianapolis Field Office conducted limited follow-up, which involved conducting a telephonic interview on September 2 of one of the three athletes, reviewing the thumb drive provided by Penny, and discussing the allegations with the U.S. Attorney's Office (USAO) in the Southern District of Indiana and the FBI's Detroit Field Office. The Indianapolis office did not formally document any of its investigative activity, including its July meeting with USA Gymnastics and its September 2 telephonic interview of one of the victim gymnasts. The office also did not formally open an investigation or assessment of the matter. The only 2015 Indianapolis Field Office documentation located by the OIG consisted of five pages of handwritten notes taken by two of the FBI attendees at the July 2015 meeting with USA Gymnastics, three pages of notes taken by the two agents at the September 2 interview of the one athlete, a handful of email exchanges between Penny and the FBI Indianapolis Field Office, and approximately 45 emails and text messages among agents and prosecutors.

In September 2015, following the September 2 interview of the victim gymnast, the Indianapolis Field Office, as well as the USAO for the Southern District of Indiana, concluded that there was no venue in Indianapolis since Indianapolis had no connection to any of the alleged illegal activity.

In other words, if the crime didn't happen there, the crime couldn't be investigated or prosecuted there.

Further, both offices had serious questions as to whether the allegations against Nassar were sufficient to support federal jurisdiction. Yet, the Indianapolis Field Office did not advise state or local authorities about the allegations and did not take any action to mitigate the risk to gymnasts that Nassar continued to treat. Instead, the Indianapolis agents and Assistant U.S. Attorney (AUSA) determined that, if the FBI had jurisdiction, venue would likely be most appropriate in the Western District of Michigan and the FBI's Lansing Resident Agency, where MSU is located and where Nassar treated patients. Accordingly, the AUSA advised the Indianapolis Field Office on September 2 to transfer the case to the FBI's Lansing Resident Agency. However, the Indianapolis Field Office failed to do so, despite informing USA Gymnastics on September 4 that it had transferred the matter to the FBI's Detroit Field Office (of which the FBI's Lansing Resident Agency is a part).

USA GYMNASTICS REPORTS SEXUAL ASSAULT ALLEGATIONS TO THE FBI'S LOS ANGELES FIELD OFFICE IN MAY 2016.

After 8 months of FBI inactivity, USA Gymnastics officials contacted the FBI's Los Angeles Field Office and met with that office in May 2016 to report the same allegations concerning Nassar that it had provided to the Indianapolis Field Office in July 2015. The Los Angeles Field Office then contacted a Supervisory Special Agent (SSA) in the Indianapolis Field Office (Indianapolis SSA) to learn what the Indianapolis office had done in response to the USA Gymnastics complaint. The Indianapolis SSA told the Los Angeles SSA that he had created a formal FBI complaint form (FD-71) in 2015 to transfer the Nassar allegations from the Indianapolis office to the Lansing Resident Agency; however, the Los Angeles Field Office, the Indianapolis SSA, and other FBI employees stated that they searched for the FD-71 in the FBI's computer system but could not find it. The OIG also found no evidence that such a document had been sent to the Lansing Resident Agency in 2015.

Following its May 2016 meeting with USA Gymnastics, the Los Angeles Field Office, in contrast to the Indianapolis Field Office, opened a federal sexual tourism investigation against Nassar and undertook numerous investigative steps, including interviewing several of Nassar's alleged victims.

However, like the Indianapolis Field Office, the Los Angeles Field Office did not reach out to any state or local authorities, even though it was aware of allegations that Nassar may have violated state laws and was unsure whether the evidence would support any federal criminal charges. It also did not take any action to mitigate the risk to gymnasts that Nassar continued to treat.

Opening a federal sexual tourism investigation is another way of saying they were looking into charging Nassar for traveling with the intent to engage in illicit sexual conduct with a child, which is punishable by up to thirty years in prison, because Nassar did travel across state lines and abroad with the national team.

THE MSU POLICE DEPARTMENT LEARNS OF NASSAR'S ALLEGED ABUSE AND EXECUTES A SEARCH WARRANT ON NASSAR'S RESIDENCE IN SEPTEMBER 2016; THE FBI LANSING RESIDENT AGENCY SUBSEQUENTLY LEARNS OF THE ALLEGATIONS.

In August 2016, the Michigan State University Police Department (MSUPD) received a separate complaint from a gymnast who stated that she was sexually assaulted by Nassar when she was 16 years old.

This was Rachael Denhollander.

Two weeks later, *The Indianapolis Star* ran a news story describing sexual assault allegations against Nassar by former gymnasts. The MSUPD then received similar sexual abuse complaints against Nassar from dozens of additional young females and, on September 20, 2016, the MSUPD executed a court-authorized search warrant at Nassar's residence and, among other things, discovered and seized electronic devices containing child pornography.

As a result of the news stories and MSUPD investigative activity, the FBI's Lansing Resident Agency first learned of the Nassar allegations and opened its Nassar investigation on October 5, 2016 (neither the FBI's Indianapolis Field Office nor the FBI's Los Angeles Field Office had previously informed the Lansing Resident Agency of the Nassar allegations). The Lansing Resident Agency ultimately discovered over 30,000 images of child pornography on the devices seized by the MSUPD during its search of Nassar's residence.

The September 2016 news reports and MSUPD investigative activity also resulted in Nassar being removed from his positions at MSU, Twistars USA Gymnastics Club, and Holt High School. According to civil court documents, approximately 70 or more young athletes were allegedly sexually abused by Nassar under the guise of medical treatment between July 2015, when USA Gymnastics first reported allegations about Nassar to the Indianapolis Field Office, and September 2016. For many of the approximately 70 or more athletes, the abuse by Nassar began before the FBI first became aware of allegations against Nassar and continued into 2016. For others, the alleged abuse began after USA Gymnastics reported the Nassar allegations to the Indianapolis Field Office in July 2015.

This is unforgivable!

NASSAR IS PROSECUTED, CONVICTED AND SENTENCED.

Nassar was arrested and charged by the Michigan Attorney General in November 2016 with multiple counts of criminal sexual conduct related to his sexual assault of gymnasts. In December 2016, the FBI arrested Nassar on federal possession of child pornography charges related to the images seized during the MSUPD's search of his residence. Nassar was not charged with child sexual tourism, the federal offense that the Indianapolis Field Office had considered and the Los Angeles Field Office had investigated.

In July 2017, Nassar pleaded guilty in federal court to Receipt and Attempted Receipt of Child Pornography, Possession of Child Pornography, and Destruction and Concealment of Records and Tangible Objects, and he was sentenced to 60 years in federal prison in December 2017. In November 2017, Nassar pleaded guilty in Michigan state court to seven counts of First Degree Criminal Sexual Conduct, and an addendum to the plea agreement indicated that there were 115 alleged victims. In January 2018, Nassar was sentenced to 40 to 175 years in Michigan state prison. In February 2018, after pleading guilty to three additional counts of criminal sexual conduct, Nassar was sentenced in Michigan state court to an additional 40 to 125 years in prison.

THE FBI IS QUESTIONED BY REPORTERS IN 2017 AND 2018 ABOUT ITS ALLEGED LACK OF INVESTIGATIVE ACTION FOLLOWING THE USA GYMNASTICS REFERRAL IN JULY 2015.

In early 2017, reporters questioned FBI and USA Gymnastics officials about the time that elapsed between when USA Gymnastics first reported the sexual assault allegations to the FBI in July 2015 and the MSUPD search of his residence in September 2016. These inquiries prompted Indianapolis Field Office Special Agent in Charge (SAC) W. Jay Abbott to propose that the FBI release a statement indicating that the FBI had expeditiously responded to the Nassar allegations (the FBI did not issue the statement) and resulted in FBI headquarters drafting a white paper (relying on Indianapolis Field Office information) that was intended to summarize the FBI's handling of the Nassar allegations but omitted critical information about the FBI's failure to timely interview the victim gymnasts.

These 2017 press questions also resulted in FBI officials discussing the Indianapolis Field Office's receipt of the Nassar allegations in 2015 and its investigative response, which the Indianapolis SSA described in an electronic communication (EC) that is dated February 1, 2017. The EC includes a claim that the Indianapolis SSA had drafted an

FD-71 report and sent it to the Lansing Resident Agency in 2015, "but to date [it] cannot be located." As noted above, the OIG found no evidence that such a report had ever been sent to the Lansing Resident Agency.

Additionally, on February 2, 2017, the Indianapolis SSA drafted an interview summary (FD-302) of the one gymnast interview he had conducted 17 months earlier in September 2015. He did so despite being told by the FBI office then handling the investigation (the Lansing Resident Agency) to not do so. In drafting the FD-302, the Indianapolis SSA used only his one page of limited notes and memory and did not consult with his FBI co-interviewer or review her notes (even though the co-interviewer had given the Indianapolis SSA her notes). The FD-302 includes statements purportedly made by the gymnast during her Indianapolis interview that she later told the OIG she did not make, that are not contained in the Indianapolis SSA's notes, that the FBI co-interviewer did not recall the gymnast making, and that conflict with statements the gymnast made during her Los Angeles Field Office interview in 2016 and USA Gymnastics interview in 2015. These statements were highly relevant to Nassar's criminal defense, and the inaccuracies included in the FD-302 by the Indianapolis SSA could have jeopardized the then-ongoing, and future, criminal investigations by providing false information to bolster Nassar's defense.

They were supposed to serve justice, but were they obstructing it instead?

Similar questions in early 2018 about the timeliness of the FBI's handling of the Nassar allegations resulted in Abbott (who had recently retired from the FBI) providing a reporter with an inaccurate statement that claimed, among other things, that "there was no delay by the FBI on this matter" and that the Indianapolis Field Office had provided a "detailed report" to both the FBI Detroit and Los Angeles Field Offices. Further, these inquiries resulted in an official with the Indianapolis Field Office proposing factually inaccurate changes to the white paper created in 2017 that sought to place blame on others, including claiming that the Indianapolis Field Office's limited efforts to interview the victim gymnasts were due to the reluctance of the gymnasts and interference by USA Gymnastics, rather than the fault of the Indianapolis Field Office.

ABBOTT ENGAGES WITH PENNY REGARDING A U.S. OLYMPIC COMMITTEE POSITION WHILE CONTINUING TO PARTICIPATE IN FBI DISCUSSIONS REGARDING THE NASSAR INVESTIGATION.

During the course of the OIG investigation, we learned that in the fall of 2015, after the Indianapolis Field Office decided to refer the Nassar allegations to the FBI's Lansing Resident Agency but while the matter was still pending at the FBI, Abbott met with Penny at a bar and discussed a potential job opportunity with the U.S. Olympic Committee. Thereafter, Abbott engaged with Penny about both his interest in the U.S. Olympic Committee position and the Nassar investigation, while at the same time participating in discussions at the FBI related to the Nassar investigation. These discussions included Penny expressing concern to Abbott about how USA Gymnastics was being portrayed in the media and whether Penny might be "in trouble" and Abbott proposing to his colleagues an FBI public statement that would place USA Gymnastics in a positive light.

At the same time, Abbott was aware that Penny appeared willing to put in a good word on Abbott's behalf in connection with the U.S.

> OMG, doesn't it look like they were trading favors?! Like they were putting their own concerns above ours? Could this also be why when my mother later urged the FBI to look into Steve Penny for the way he had mishandled the reporting of my abuse and others', she was told the agents were directed to investigate only Nassar?

Olympic Committee job. Abbott applied for the U.S. Olympic Committee position in 2017 but was not selected. Despite evidence confirming that Abbott had applied for the job, Abbott denied to the OIG during two interviews that he had applied for the position and told the OIG that applying for the job would have presented a conflict of interest.

RESULTS OF THE INVESTIGATION

The OIG found that, despite the extraordinarily serious nature of the allegations and the possibility that Nassar's conduct could be continuing, senior officials in the FBI Indianapolis Field Office failed to respond to the Nassar allegations with the utmost seriousness and urgency that they deserved and required, made numerous and fundamental errors when they did respond to them, and violated multiple FBI policies. The Indianapolis Field Office did not undertake any investigative activity until September 2—5 weeks after the meeting with USA Gymnastics—when they telephonically interviewed one of the three athletes. Further, FBI Indianapolis never interviewed the other two gymnasts who they were told were available to meet with FBI investigators.

This absence of any serious investigative activity was compounded when the Indianapolis Field Office did not transfer the matter to the FBI office (the Lansing Resident Agency), where venue most likely would have existed had evidence been developed to support the potential federal crimes being considered, even though the Indianapolis office had been advised to do so by the USAO and had told USA Gymnastics that the transfer had occurred. As a result, the Lansing Resident Agency did not learn of the Nassar allegations until over a year after they were first reported to the FBI and then learned of them only from the MSUPD. Moreover, the FBI conducted no investigative activity in the matter for more than 8 months following the September 2015 interview, and only then did so after USA Gymnastics brought the Nassar allegations to the FBI's Los Angeles Field Office due to the lack of investigative activity.

Additionally, the Indianapolis office did not notify state or local authorities of the sexual assault allegations even though it questioned whether there was federal jurisdiction to pursue them. It also took no action to mitigate the ongoing threat that Nassar presented to the gymnasts he was continuing to treat and, as alleged and detailed in numerous civil complaints, Nassar's sexual assaults continued.

Further, when the FBI's handling of the Nassar matter came under scrutiny from the public, Congress, the media, and FBI headquarters in 2017 and 2018, Indianapolis officials did not take responsibility for their failures. Instead, they provided incomplete and inaccurate information in response to FBI internal inquiries (and Abbott, after he retired, provided inaccurate information to the media) to make it appear that the Indianapolis office had been diligent in its follow-up efforts and they did so, in part, by blaming others for their own failures.

The OIG identified multiple failures and policy violations by the Indianapolis Field Office in connection with its handling of the Nassar allegations. Among other things, the OIG found that the Indianapolis Field Office did not properly document the July 2015 meeting with USA Gymnastics, the Indianapolis SSA failed to properly handle and document receipt and review of the thumb drive provided by USA Gymnastics during the July 2015 meeting, the Indianapolis SSA did not document the September 2015 victim interview alleging criminal sexual assault by Nassar in an FD-302 report until 17 months after the interview occurred, the FD-302 of the September 2015 victim interview that was drafted by the Indianapolis SSA in February 2017 included materially false information and omitted material information, and the FBI Indianapolis Field Office did not coordinate with state or local authorities although it believed that the allegations it received likely did not fall within federal jurisdiction. In addition, although the Indianapolis SSA told the OIG that he completed and forwarded an FD-71 complaint form in the FBI's electronic case management system to the FBI's Lansing Resident Agency, we determined that an FD-71 form never reached the Lansing Resident Agency and the Indianapolis SSA, the FBI Inspection Division, and other FBI employees stated they could not find an FD-71 in the FBI's case management system or elsewhere.

The OIG also found that, while the FBI Los Angeles Field Office appreciated the utmost seriousness of the Nassar allegations and took numerous investigative steps upon learning of them in May 2016, the office also did not expeditiously notify local law enforcement or the FBI Lansing Resident Agency of the information that it had learned or take other action to mitigate the ongoing danger that Nassar posed. Indeed, precisely because of its investigative activity, the Los Angeles Field Office was aware from interviewing multiple witnesses that Nassar's abuse was potentially widespread and that there were specific allegations of sexual assault against him for his actions while at the Karolyi Training Camp (also known as the Karolyi Ranch) in Huntsville, Texas. Yet, the Los Angeles Field Office did not contact the Sheriff's Office in Walker County, Texas, to provide it with the information that it had developed until after the MSUPD had taken action against Nassar in September 2016. Nor did it have any contact with the FBI Lansing Resident Agency until after the Lansing Resident Agency first learned about the Nassar allegations from the MSUPD and public news reporting. Given the continuing threat posed by Nassar, the uncertainty over whether the Los Angeles Field Office had venue over the allegations, and the doubt that there was even federal jurisdiction to charge the sexual tourism crime that the Los Angeles Field Office was seeking to pursue, we found that prudence and sound judgment dictated that the Los Angeles Field Office should have notified local authorities upon developing the serious evidence of sexual assault against Nassar that its investigative actions were uncovering.

In addition, we concluded that the Indianapolis SSA, in an effort to minimize or excuse his errors, made false statements during two OIG-compelled interviews regarding his interview of one of Nassar's victims. Similarly, we found that Abbott, in an effort to minimize or excuse his own and his office's actions, falsely asserted in two separate OIG interviews that he communicated with both the Detroit SAC and the Los Angeles SAC about the Nassar allegations and sent ECs to both field offices in the fall of 2015. We found no evidence to support these claims.

Separately, the OIG found that Abbott violated the FBI's conflicts of interest policy by meeting with Penny to discuss the U.S. Olympic Committee job and later communicating with Penny about the job opportunity in the midst of the other communications and the proposed FBI public statement described above. We further found that, under federal ethics regulations, Abbott exercised extremely poor judgment by failing to consult with a designated agency ethics official regarding his ongoing involvement in Nassar investigation discussions at the same time he was seeking Penny's help and guidance about a U.S. Olympic Committee job opportunity. Abbott should have known—and in fact did know according to the evidence we found—that his actions would raise a question regarding his impartiality. We further concluded that Abbott made false statements to the OIG about the job discussion, his application for the position, and his handling of the Nassar allegations.

The Department declined prosecution of Abbott and the Indianapolis SSA in September 2020. Following these declinations, the OIG was able to compel interviews of the Indianapolis SSA and eight other FBI witnesses who had declined voluntary interviews and whom we were previously unable to compel to participate in interviews due to the ongoing criminal investigation and their Fifth Amendment privilege against self-incrimination. Following these interviews, we were able to complete our administrative investigation, which resulted in the findings detailed above. In addition, on May 14, 2021, the Department notified the OIG that it was not opening a new matter to investigate whether the Indianapolis SSA made false statements during his compelled OIG interviews.

The Inspector General went on to detail recommendations, some of which were already being instituted at the FBI. While these changes are good measures and we know that Inspector Horowitz has done all that he could in his position, as his role is primarily to investigate and present what happened, the failures at the FBI were *not* necessarily due to policies or procedures that needed to change, as much as they were due to people who had ignored and circumvented existing policies and procedures. My statement, which was given before Mr. Horowitz's that day, appears below, and the questions I asked then remain to this day. I don't think I will stop asking them until we get some answers, because without knowing *why* things went so horribly wrong, without knowing why these people acted against all their training, and without making a public example of them, something like this could potentially happen again. As my father has said, "Nassar was basically the gun in the crime. He was the weapon. We got rid of the weapon, but what about the people who left the weapon out in the open or who looked the other way while it was being fired at will?"

MAGGIE NICHOLS'S STATEMENT SEPTEMBER 15, 2021, JUDICIARY COMMITTEE HEARING

Chair Durbin, Ranking Member Grassley, and distinguished members of the Judiciary Committee. Thank you for inviting me to speak to you today, and I want to personally thank you for your commitments to prioritizing athlete safety and holding accountable those responsible for athlete safety.

I was named as Gymnast 2 in the Office of Inspector General's report and previously identified as Athlete A by USA Gymnastics. I want everyone to know that this did not happen to Gymnast 2 or to Athlete A. It happened to me, Maggie Nichols.

I first started gymnastics when I was [3] and since I was a child, I always had the dream of competing for my country in the World Championships and Olympic Games. I was an elite level gymnast by the age of 13, and by the time I was 14, I made the National Team. I traveled internationally for four (4) years attending competitions and in 2015 competed at the World Championships representing our country, where I won a Gold medal. My Olympic dreams ended in the summer of 2015, when my coach and I reported Larry Nassar's abuse to USAG leadership. I went on to compete at the University of Oklahoma, where I was named First Team All-American in the all-around and all four events and was a Two-Time National Champion.

I reported my abuse to USA Gymnastics over six years ago, and still, my family and I have received few answers, and have even more questions, about how this was allowed to occur and why dozens of other little girls and women at Michigan State had to be abused after I reported. In sacrificing my childhood for the chance to compete for the United States, I am haunted by the fact that even after I reported my abuse, so many women and girls had to needlessly suffer at the hands of Larry Nassar. USA Gymnastics, the United States Olympic & Paralympic Committee[,] and the FBI have all betrayed me and those who were abused by Larry Nassar after I reported.

The cover-up of my abuse, and the FBI's failure to interview me for more than a year after my complaint, are well documented in the OIG report. After I reported my abuse to USA Gymnastics, my family and I were told[,] by their former President Steve Penny, to keep quiet and not say anything that could hurt the FBI investigation. We now know there was no real FBI investigation occurring. While my complaints languished with the FBI, Larry Nassar continued to abuse women and girls. During this time, the FBI issued no search warrants, and made no arrests. From the day I reported my molestation by Nassar, I was treated differently by USAG.

Not only did the FBI fail to conduct a thorough investigation, but they also knew that USAG and the USOPC created a false narrative where Larry Nassar was allowed to "retire" with his reputation intact and return to Michigan State University; thus, allowing dozens of little girls to be molested. As the Inspector General's Report details, during this same period, FBI agents did not properly document evidence, failed to report to proper authorities, and the Special Agent in charge was seeking to become the new director of security for the United States Olympic & Paralympic Committee; a job opportunity raised by Steve Penny. Afterwards, FBI agents in charge of the investigation, lied to OIG investigators about what had occurred. This conduct by these FBI agents, including the Special Agent In-Charge, who are held in high regard and expected to protect the public, is unacceptable, disgusting, and shameful.

This committee produced a report in 2019 titled *The Courage of Survivors—A Call to Action*. It found that "the U.S. Olympic Committee and USAG, the National Governing Body designated by USOC to administer amateur gymnastics— failed to adequately respond to credible allegations against Nassar." Similarly, the OIG report found that senior FBI officials lied to the Inspector General, engaged in serious conflicts of interest, and tried to cover up one of the biggest child sexual abuse scandals in the history of amateur sports. Both reports uncovered serious and possibly criminal misconduct by those at the highest level of the Olympic Committee, our sport, and the FBI.

Despite these findings of serious and criminal misconduct throughout the FBI, USAG[,] and USOPC, no accountability has occurred. An important question remains, perhaps the most important question: [W]hy? Why would the FBI agents lie to OIG investigators? Why would the FBI not properly document evidence that was received? Why would an FBI agent be interested in the [position of USOC Chief Security Officer]? These questions remain unanswered, and the survivors of Larry Nassar have a right to know why their well-being was placed in jeopardy by these individuals who chose not to do their jobs.

[To date,] no one from the FBI, the USOPC[,] or USAG has faced federal charges, other than Larry Nassar. For many hundreds of survivors of Larry Nassar, this hearing is one of our last opportunities to get justice. We ask that you do what is in your power to ensure those that engaged in wrongdoing are held accountable under the law.

As of the writing of this chapter, almost a year after that hearing, we have still not received a satisfactory explanation, and it appears as if those involved in wrongdoing at the FBI have managed to evade legal consequences.

There are theories about why USA Gymnastics was slow to bring our allegations to the authorities in the first place. The Olympics, as it happens, are more than a point of pride for top medal-winning nations. Over the years, they have become big money makers, so the fear of any kind of negative press is real. In 2016, before the news about Nassar hit, USA Gymnastics generated $34 million in revenue, a significant portion of which came from sponsorships. Sure enough, during the lead-up to the Nassar sentencing hearing in 2018, all the negative media coverage, and the nature of the allegations themselves, led to a mass exodus of corporate partners. AT&T, Proctor & Gamble, and Kellogg's all declined to renew their deals until the organization could put better protections in place for their athletes. But there was even more money at stake than that. In the summer of 2015, not too long after I reported Nassar, Boston dropped its bid to host the Olympics in 2024 and Los Angeles stepped up to bid instead. By this point there were just two cities in the running: LA and Paris. It stands to reason that USA Gymnastics didn't want the growing problems with Larry Nassar to be the cause of the USOC losing that bid. The Olympics have traditionally boosted the economies of the host city, and by extension, the host nation. A potential news leak about an investigation into systemic sexual abuse at a US Olympic training organization at any point in the bidding process could have cost US commerce a lot of money. LA ultimately won the bid to host the Olympics in 2028, as the bids for both 2024 and 2028 were held simultaneously. Revenues from the weeks-long event are expected to top 11 billion dollars.

By contrast, the FBI's reasons for behaving as they did are still unclear. (Also unclear are the reasons why all my mother's correspondences with the FBI mysteriously disappeared from her phone one day.) But it's become vitally important that we deal with this issue now. A lot of time has passed since Nassar's sentencing in 2018. The misimpression that the whole scandal has been resolved is lodged in people's minds even though many who played a part have still not been held to task. When the public's attention is diverted, justice can sometimes falter, and we can't let that happen.

We were surprised in April of 2022 when evidence-tampering charges against Steve Penny, who had been out on bail awaiting trial, were suddenly dropped. The DA said it was due to insufficient evidence. My lawyer questioned this decision openly in a letter to Will Durham, the Walker County district attorney, stating that at no time did Durham ever suggest to us that he didn't have the evidence to try Penny. In fact, Durham reiterated that he felt the case was strong and important to try given the damage done by Penny's conduct.

We cannot let the FBI's failings go unaddressed in court too. That is why in June of 2022, Simone Biles, McKayla Maroney, Aly Raisman, and I filed Collective Administrative Claims against the FBI for their mishandling of the credible complaints of sexual assault by Larry Nassar they received in July of 2015. The Federal Tort Claims Act (FTCA) provides a legal means for compensating individuals who have suffered personal injury caused by the negligent or wrongful act or omission of the federal government, which as the Inspector General's own report suggests was the case here. Among those joining us in the claims are ninety young women and girls who were abused *after* 2015 due to the FBI's failure to protect them.

The safety of the athletes who bring us so much national pride (and all those striving to be like them) should never come at a price—*any* price— ever again. Success definitely requires sacrifices. I gave up a lot in my youth because I was so focused on becoming one of the top gymnasts in the world. Training was often hard. Powering through physical and emotional injury took a lot from me. My family also made sacrifices. **The truth is, being very** successful at something is going to exact a cost, but it should never rob you of your integrity, your agency, or your right to be protected from predatory behavior of any kind.

This is a lesson I will continue to deliver whenever and wherever I can. It is why I will see things through to their end. Why we are pursuing answers and damages from the FBI. Why I will continue to tell my story. Why I hope it inspires others. Why I will try to close out the unfinished business of this case. Why I got my master's degree to help others. Why I will continue to support the protection of young people everywhere.

And while I am doing all these things, I will also continue to set and achieve new and exciting goals for myself in other areas of my life, working to be the best that I can be at those things too, knowing they will require some sacrifices as well—sacrifices of *my* choosing.

CHAPTER FIFTEEN
REFLECTION

Your life does not get better by
chance; it gets better by change.

—JIM ROHN

Immediately after graduation, I headed to South Padre Island in Texas to relax, celebrate, and contemplate my next steps. I had received several job offers and wanted to give each of them careful consideration.

I was preparing for another knee surgery as well. I will likely have to replace my knee with an artificial one in the future, but since I am still so young, the plan was to have a procedure called an osteotomy in the interim. To alleviate the pain of bone grating on bone, this surgery involves cutting and realigning part of the tibia (aka the shinbone) or the femur (aka the thigh bone) to relieve pressure on the joint. In a healthy knee, your weight is equally distributed between the outer and inner part of the joint. When you've had multiple injuries to the knee, as I've had, an osteotomy helps redistribute the weight away from the damaged part. I ultimately had this surgery in December of 2022 and am happy to say it went well. It was an invasive procedure, so as I write this chapter, it is still taking time to heal, but I look forward to being my optimal best soon.

Just after graduation, I had also begun a speaking tour and wanted to add a few more thoughts to my talk. I absolutely love addressing young people at campuses and community events nationwide. It is an important part of my mission going forward.

The We Are Strong Invitational Tour with Maggie Nichols is another of my passions that I now get to spend more time on. We hold women's gymnastics competitions in five major cities with an emphasis on team bonding and togetherness. These competitions are open to USA Gymnastics, NGA levels 1–10, and Xcel divisions, and are designed to restore the true meaning and purpose of gymnastics in our athletes' lives.

In addition, I wanted to use my time away to reflect more broadly. My training in the gym taught me to think about what I am supposed to learn from the significant events that happened to me, whether it was a success, an injury, a defeat, or a disappointment. Life is a pretty big classroom, so I'm sure I'll continue learning, but ending the formal education chapter of my life seemed like the right time to stop and think about the lessons I want to take forward with me.

These last six years of my life, more so than any other time, have emphasized the importance of unity and teamwork. When you leave school, especially a school where you participated in athletics, that formal structure is gone. It got me thinking about how to take that mentality into the larger world, and I think we do that just by being more mindful—by treating everyone around us as part of a larger team.

The experiences I have written about in this book point to the fact that the adults who failed us weren't concerned with *the other*, while the adults who had our backs were. Sarah Jantzi was definitely on Team Athlete, more specifically Team Maggie. She was mindful and picked up on signs and behaviors around her. She did more than just notice; she asked questions and acted on her instincts to protect me and other girls.

The journalistic team at the *IndyStar*, as well as then Detective Sergeant

Andrea Munford, then Assistant Attorney General Angela Povilaitis, Judge Rosemarie Aquilina, and attorney John Manly have all pursued fields where they mind us professionally. The very best coaches, like those at TCT and OU, know to do that too.

But *all of us* can be minders of each other on a personal, day-to-day basis. If something is happening to you, you can assume it is happening to someone else. When you feel vulnerable, stay alert, ask questions, be curious. Find those other people experiencing the same thing and work together to correct the situation. I am grateful to be working with my former national teammates to make a difference in how girls and young women are treated in sports and how sexual abuse survivors are treated in the justice system.

The team we all should be playing for is society. We were all born to that team, and all the positions have the same goal, which is to look out for one another. We win when we are all treated with respect and care. The takeaway is not a trophy that gets displayed behind glass; it is the same sense of belonging and safety I felt when I was competing with my Sooner teammates.

When we are in college, we spend a lot of time deciding *what* we want to be after graduation. Let's spend more time deciding *who* we want to be, because how we act in our communities is even more important than any job we will ever hold. This whole experience has me committed to the team . . . and I hope that after reading this book, you will be too.

The other lesson I know I will carry with me into the future has to do with disappointment and how to deal with it effectively. Being disappointed is an inevitable part of life. Some disappointments are way worse than others. Some are downright injustices. But honestly, there is no point in wallowing in them. I mean it. Wallowing just prolongs the situation. It's counterproductive. Strong people resist the urge to throw a pity party. They come out of disappointment fighting. They don't play the victim or play the blame game. They cope by moving on. They look forward, not backward, unless it's for clarity. And when they share their experience, they hope to inspire and help others avoid the same fate. They don't whine. They would much rather be known for all the good things they do than for the time they got screwed. That's how you handle disappointment with dignity and integrity. How you clear the path for recovery and success. And how you triumph in the long run. Just saying.

SEXUAL ABUSE RESOURCES

I recently established the Maggie Nichols Foundation, a nonprofit organization whose mission is to assist charities that help heal victims and survivors of all types of abuse. Together we can make a positive difference and can empower survivors. I look forward to sharing more about the foundation soon, so be sure to visit our website at **we-are-strong.org**.

Also be sure to check out the Rape, Abuse & Incest National Network (aka **RAINN**) at **rainn.org/national-resources-sexual-assault-survivors -and-their-loved-ones**. As the nation's largest anti–sexual violence organization, they offer well-developed victim-centered, trauma-informed services to survivors of sexual violence and their loved ones at every stage of recovery. In addition, they also provide public education and influence public policy, creating and advocating for laws and regulations that make communities safer and support survivors. Note that their National Sexual Assault Hotline is accessible 24/7 by **phone** (**800.656.HOPE**) and **online** (**online.rainn.org**).

WARNING SIGNS

Throughout Larry Nassar's career, every time allegations were made, there were people who were willing to give him, and not the victim, the benefit of the doubt. It is true that you are innocent until proven guilty, but even in the face of mounting incriminating evidence, some still maintained that his practices were medically sound. It is why Amanda Thomashow's case in 2014, which is referred to in chapter 9, was never picked up by the prosecutor's office. The Title IX review of her claims determined that Larry's medical treatment was appropriate.

USA Gymnastics and the FBI also gave Nassar far more leeway than they did the victims. I am all for doing due diligence—thoroughly investigating before charging someone with such a serious crime—but as time drew on, it sure seemed as if some were more concerned with protecting the medical license of a supposedly reputable doctor than they were with providing safety for the young girls he was treating.

The fact that Nassar employed one common remedy for the widely different ailments athletes came to him with should have been a huge red flag, especially because that remedy consistently involved inappropriate touching of the genital region or the breasts. Interviews with survivors indicated that if an athlete came in with a back problem, a hip problem, a hamstring problem, or restricted flexibility, he did an "intravaginal adjustment." He would claim that massaging a pressure point there would alleviate pain, or realign their joints, or that it was the easiest way to stretch muscles without pain. As a guise for attending to an issue with the ribs, shoulder, or other upper body parts, he would also touch athletes' breasts. He used various medical terms and principles to mask what he was doing. Among the most common principles was that of "myofascial continuity"—the notion that tightness in one muscle group can lead to corresponding looseness in another. Essentially, by claiming everything is connected, he could work his hands wherever he wanted to. A knee injury could lead him to attending to your back, all through the pelvic floor.

It is also troubling that the thumb drive containing a presentation Nassar frequently made at conferences wasn't a huge red flag for FBI agents and others who viewed it. It bizarrely used Star Trek references. For example, its opening lines read, "These are the voyages of the 'Sports Pelvic Floor' specialist whose lifetime mission . . . to boldly go where no man has gone before (in most of our young gymnasts—hopefully)." This is a classic case of someone hiding their crimes in plain sight. He was bragging about his exploits while showing others his "technique" for alleviating pain, which actually was a technique for inflicting pain—psychic, emotional, and physical pain—in the athletes he treated.

I have debated about being too specific or graphic in this book, but I decided to share the above details with you because education is our best defense. To protect yourself in any situation that feels uncomfortable to you, please remember the following:

1. Your doctor should never touch you in ways that make you feel uncomfortable. Procedures should be explained to you in advance. You should also be given an opportunity to ask questions and to consent or decline as you wish.

2. If at any time before or during a medical treatment you would like to have a chaperone present, such as a same-sex nurse, you should ask for one. This is true of any treatment, but especially an examination or treatment involving a sensitive area, such as your private parts. If a doctor denies your request, leave. Having a chaperone present protects you against any inappropriate behavior and protects the doctor against any unfounded claims. A reputable doctor will want to do whatever is appropriate to put you at ease and to effectively treat you at the same time.

3. A reputable doctor never uses sexual innuendo or makes sexual jokes with a patient. Several of Nassar's survivors reported him talking about sexually explicit topics with them and even joking that they should try

what he was doing with their boyfriend. That is *never* appropriate.

4. Your doctor should provide proper covering for you. You should feel free to ask that the treatment be done over clothing if that is possible and makes you feel more comfortable. Your body parts should not be exposed during examination or treatment. There were some instances when Nassar covered his patients with a towel to mask what he was doing. Even if a covering is provided, you should still ask for a chaperone to be present if the treated area is a sensitive one, and that chaperone should have full view of what the doctor is doing.

5. Similarly, skin-to-skin contact should be minimized, and if a doctor must perform a pelvic exam for any legitimate reason, surgical gloves should always be worn. The fact that Nassar was not wearing them was a red flag for me and should be for you too.

6. Appointments should be scheduled during regular business hours. Another red flag is being asked to come very late in the day when other staff members are getting ready to leave or have already gone home.

7. And lastly, if your doctor has pictures of famous patients in their office or on social media without their patients' consent, beware. That is a HIPPA violation. It means that doctor will likely not respect your privacy either. Nassar's walls were covered with gymnasts' photos. This misuse of his celebrity patients' images fostered a trust between him and his other patients that he did not earn, and in some ways those photos were tools in grooming those girls.

Awareness can be empowering *for us all.* Those of you who are involved in sports and are seeing trainers, physical therapists, and doctors on a regular basis should be especially conscious of these warning signs and what to do about them.

By the way, Nassar's "medical defense" was finally debunked when one young woman who was *not* part of the gymnastics world joined the rest of us survivors with her own account of abuse by Larry Nassar. Kyle Stephens's parents were close friends with Nassar and his wife throughout her childhood. She had been repeatedly molested by Larry in the basement of his home from the time she was six years old. When she told her parents what was happening, they confronted Nassar, but he denied the claims, and sadly he was believed. Fortunately, Kyle's account was contemporaneously documented in sessions with her therapist, serving later as evidence. Because Kyle was *not* a gymnast and she was *not* seeking physical therapy from Nassar, what he did to her could *not* be dismissed as "medical treatment." When she came forward as a young adult, her experience seriously called into question whether Nassar was really administering pain relief to all of us girls all those other times.

MAGGIE NICHOLS
OFFICIAL RECORD

CAREER HIGHLIGHTS

- 2020 AAI Award Winner
- 2019 NCAA team, all-around & vault champion and uneven bars silver medalist (Oklahoma)
- 2018 NCAA all-around, uneven bars & floor exercise champion and team & balance beam silver medalist (Oklahoma)
- 2017 NCAA team & uneven bars champion (Oklahoma)
- 2016 American Cup silver medalist
- 2015 World team champion and floor exercise bronze medalist
- 2015 US all-around silver medalist
- 2014 US all-around, uneven bars & floor exercise bronze medalist

NATIONAL COMPETITION RESULTS

- 2019 NCAA Women's Gymnastics Championships, Fort Worth, Tex.: 1st-Team, AA, VT(T); 2nd-UB(T); 6th-BB(T); 7th-FX(T)
- 2018 NCAA Women's Gymnastics Championships, St. Louis, Mo.: 1st-AA, UB(T), FX(T); 2nd-Team, BB(T); 6th-VT(T)
- 2017 NCAA Women's Gymnastics Championships, St. Louis, Mo.: 1st-Team, UB(T); 8th-VT(T)
- 2016 US Olympic Team Trials, San Jose, Calif.: 4th-FX; 5th-VT; 6th-AA; 8th-BB
- 2016 P&G Championships, St. Louis, Mo.
- 2015 P&G Championships, Indianapolis, Ind.: 2nd-AA; 4th-BB(T); 5th-FX; 7th-UB

- 2015 Secret US Classic, Chicago, Ill.: 3rd-AA, FX(T); 5th-UB, BB(T)
- 2014 P&G Championships, Pittsburgh, Pa.: 3rd-AA, UB, FX; 4th-BB
- 2014 Secret US Classic, Chicago, Ill.: 3rd-AA, FX; 5th-UB; 7th-BB
- 2013 P&G Championships, Hartford, Conn.: 5th-AA, BB; 6th-UB
- 2013 Secret US Classic, Chicago, Ill.: 5th-FX; 6th-AA; 8th-BB
- 2012 Visa Championships, St. Louis, Mo.: (Jr. Div.)
- 2012 Secret US Classic, Chicago, Ill.: 7th-VT (Jr. Div.)
- 2012 American Classic, Huntsville, Tex.: 2nd-BB(T); 3rd-AA, VT; 4th-UB(T); 7th-FX (Jr. 1)
- 2011 American Classic, Huntsville, Tex.: 2nd-BB; 3rd-VT; 8th-AA (Jr. 2)
- 2011 Elite Qualifier, Orlando, Fla.: 1st-AA, VT; 2nd-UB; 3rd-BB; 5th-FX (Jr. Div.)
- 2011 Women's Junior Olympic Level 10 National Championships, Long Beach, Calif.: 1st-UB(T), BB(T); 2nd-AA, VT; 3rd-FX(T) (Jr. A)
- 2011 Nastia Liukin Supergirl Cup, Jacksonville, Fla.
- 2010 Women's Junior Olympic Level 10 National Championships, Dallas, Tex.: 2nd-FX(T); 5th-AA, UB (Jr. A)
- 2009 CoverGirl Classic, Des Moines, Iowa: 5th-AA (Jr. Div.)
- 2009 Women's Junior Olympic Level 10 National Championships, Puyallup, Wash.: 1st-UB; 5th-FX(T); 7th-AA(T) (Jr. A)

INTERNATIONAL COMPETITION RESULTS

- 2016 AT&T American Cup, Newark, N.J.: 2nd-AA
- 2015 World Championships, Glasgow, Great Britain: 1st-Team; 3rd-FX
- 2015 Jesolo Trophy, Jesolo, Italy: 1st-Team; 7th-AA
- 2014 Pan American Championships, Toronto, Canada: 1st-Team; 3rd-AA

- 2014 Tokyo World Cup, Tokyo, Japan: 3rd-AA
- 2014 City of Jesolo Trophy, Jesolo, Italy: 1st-Team; 3rd-AA
- 2013 Mexican Open, Acapulco, Mexico: 2nd-AA (exhibition)
- 2013 USA, Germany, Romania Tri-Meet, Chemnitz, Germany: 1st-Team; 4th-AA
- 2013 City of Jesolo Trophy, Jesolo, Italy: 1st-Team; 2nd-FX; 6th-AA

COLLEGE CAREER DETAILS:

2020 (SENIOR)

Big 12 Gymnast of the Year . . . Five-time first-team WCGA All-American . . . Five-time All–Big 12 selection (vault, bars, beam, floor, all-around) . . . AAU Sullivan Award Semifinalist . . . Ranked No. 1 in the all-around and on vault to end the season . . . Finished the year ranked No. 2 on bars . . . Tallied five perfect 10.0s on the season to bring her career total to 22 . . . Ranks fourth all-time for career perfect 10.0s in NCAA history . . . Six-time Big 12 Gymnast of the Week . . . Tallied a season-high 39.900 in the all-around (Jan. 20) and is the only gymnast in NCAA history with multiple marks of 39.900 or higher . . . Secured 28 event titles, including six on vault, seven on bars, five on beam, five on floor, and five in the all-around . . . Competed in 10 of 11 meets for the Sooners . . . Tallied a 9.9 or higher on 31 of 34 routines . . . Tallied a 9.9 or higher on all 10 bar routines . . . Recorded four perfect marks on vault and one on bars . . . Earned a 39.625 or better in the all-around six times . . . Finished with the top three all-around scores in the nation with a 39.900, 39.850, and 39.825.

2019 (JUNIOR)

NCAA All-Around Champion . . . NCAA Co-Vault Champion . . . Just the sixth gymnast in NCAA history to win the all-around title in back-to-back seasons . . . Honda Sport Award Finalist . . . NCAA Inspiration Award Winner . . . Five-time first-team All-American (vault, bars, beam, floor, all-around) . . . 2019 Big 12 Beam Champion . . . 2019 Big 12 Co-Bars Champion . . . 2019 Athens Regional Bar and Vault Champion . . . WCGA First-Team All-American (bars, beam) . . . Tallied a perfect 10.0 on vault in the first meet of the season (Jan. 5) . . . Scored a perfect 10.0 on bars at the Athens Regional . . . Two-time All–Big 12 (bars, beam) . . . Two-time Big 12 Event Specialist of the Week (Jan. 28, Mar. 3) . . . Competed in 15 of 17 meets for the Sooners . . . notched a 9.9 or better on bars in every meet . . . Tallied a 9.9 or better in 13 of 15 meets on beam . . . Notched a 9.9 or higher on 36 of 40 routines she competed . . . Secured 22 event titles, including nine on beam, eight on bars, two in the all-around and vault, and one on floor.

2018 (SOPHOMORE)

NCAA Individual National Champion in the All-Around (39.8125) . . . NCAA Co-Individual National Champion on bars with a perfect 10.0 . . . NCAA Co-Individual National Champion on floor with a 9.9625 . . . First-team All-American (bars, beam, floor, all-around) . . . Second-team All-American (vault) . . . NCAA runner-up on beam with a 9.950 . . . Became just the third gymnast in OU history to record five All-America honors in one season . . . Scored a 10.0 on bars in Semifinal II, becoming just the third gymnast to ever record a 10.0 on the event at the NCAA Championships . . . NACGC/W First-Team All-American (all-around, vault, bars, beam, floor) . . . Scored eight 10.0s in her sophomore campaign (vault [twice], bars, beam [four times], floor) . . . Recorded a "Gym Slam" with a perfect 10.0 on every event for the second straight season . . . Is the only gymnast to ever record two "Gym Slams" . . . Scored two 10.0s in a meet for the first time in her career against Michigan (Mar. 3) . . . 2018 South Central Region Gymnast of the Year . . . Five-time All–Big 12 (all-around, vault, bars, beam, floor) . . . Only second gymnast in Big 12 history to earn all five awards in multiple seasons and first to do it in back-to-back years . . . 2018 Big 12 Gymnast of the Year . . . Seven-time Big 12 Gymnast of the

Week . . . Big 12 All-Around and Co-Floor Champion . . . Competed all-around in 14 of 15 meets . . . Won 45 event titles, including at least 5 on every event (all-around: 13; vault: 5; bars: 9; beam: 9; floor: 9).

2017 (FRESHMAN)

Three-Time First-Team All-American (vault, bars, floor) . . . Co-Individual National Champion on bars with a 9.95 . . . One of four finalists for the Honda Sport Award . . . NACGC/W First-Team All-American (all-around, vault, bars, beam, floor) . . . Only gymnast in the country to earn five regular season All-American accolades . . . Scored seven 10.0s in her freshman campaign (vault [twice], bars, beam [three times], floor), completing her "Gym Slam" with a perfect score on bars at Michigan on Mar. 4 . . . Ninth collegiate gymnast to post a 10.0 on all four events in a career and first since Florida's Bridget Sloan in 2015 . . . Set OU record for career 10.0s, passing Haley Scaman (five total—three on floor, two on vault) . . . Scored a 10.0 on beam during the Super Six, just the fourth 10.0 ever scored on the event at the NCAA Championships and the first earned in the team finals . . . Set OU's all-around program record with a 39.925 at the GymQuarters Mardi Gras Invitational on Feb. 17, scoring a 10.0 on beam and a trio of 9.975s on vault, bars, and floor . . . 2017 South Central Region Gymnast of the Year . . . Five-time All–Big 12 (all-around, vault, bars, beam, floor) . . . Fifth gymnast in Big 12 history to earn honors on all four events and in the all-around . . . 2017 Big 12 Newcomer of the Year . . . Big 12 Vault and Co-Bars Champion . . . 10-time Big 12 Weekly Award Winner (Gymnast of the Week—Jan. 23, Jan. 30, Feb. 20; Newcomer of the Week—Jan. 9, Jan. 16, Jan. 30, Feb. 6, Feb. 13, Mar. 6, Mar. 13) . . . Her 10 weekly honors are the most in a single season in Big 12 history, passing OU's Kiara Redmond-Sturns, who had seven in 2008 . . . Secured 45 event titles, including eight on vault, 11 on bars, 8 on beam, 9 on floor, and 9 in the all-around . . . Scored at least a 9.9 a total of 45 times this season, only posting a mark below the total four times . . . Competed all-around in first seven meets of season before resting and returning to all four events at the NCAA Seattle Regional.

CLUB/HIGH SCHOOL

Elite-level gymnast at Twin City Twisters . . . Trained under coaches Mike Hunger, Sami Wozney, Sarah Jantzi, and Rich Stenger . . . Has a wealth of national and international experience . . . Member of the 2015 US Women's World Championships team that claimed a gold medal and also earned an individual bronze medal on the floor . . . Competed on all four events in team finals at the World Championships . . . Placed sixth at 2016 US Olympic Team Trials . . . Four-time participant at the P&G Championships, securing a runner-up finish in the all-around in 2015 . . . Also tied for fourth on beam, fifth on floor, and seventh on bars at P&G in 2015 . . . Other national competition appearances include American Cup (2016, second in all-around), Secret US Classic (2012, 2013, 2014, 2015), Visa Championships (2012), American Classic (2011, 2012), Elite Qualifier (2011), Women's Junior Olympic Level 10 National Championships (2009, 2010, 2011), Nastia Liukin Supergirl Cup (2011), and CoverGirl Classic (2009) . . . Participated at Jesolo Trophy in 2013, 2014, and 2015, placing first as a team in each of those years . . . Individual finishes at Jesolo Trophy: 2013—second on floor, sixth in all-around; 2014—third in all-around; 2015—seventh in all-around . . . Finished first as a team and third individually in the all-around at 2014 Pan American Championships . . . Placed third in all-around at 2014 Tokyo World Cup . . . Earned second in the all-around in exhibition at 2013 Mexican Open . . . Member of the USA team that placed first in the 2013 USA, Germany, Romania Tri-Meet, where she also placed fourth in the all-around . . . High scores from precollegiate competition at Elite level: vault—15.95, bars—14.95, beam—14.95, floor—15.3.

CAREER PERFECT 10.0 SUMMARY

YEAR	DATE	APPARATUS	OPPONENTS	MEET DESCRIPTION
2017	Sat., Jan. 21	VT	@ West Virginia	(A)
	Fri., Feb. 03	BB	vs. Denver, Nebraska, Texas Woman's	(H)
	Fri., Feb. 10	FX	@ Auburn	(A) Perfect 10 Challenge
	Fri., Feb. 17	BB	vs. Georgia, LSU, Missouri	(H) GymQuarters Invitational
	Sat., Mar. 04	UB	@ Michigan	(A)
	Sat., Mar. 18	VT	vs. Denver, Iowa State, West Virginia	(A) Big 12 Championships
	Fri., Apr. 15	BB	Alabama, Florida, LSU, UCLA, Utah	(A) NCAA Championships Super Six
2018	Sun., Feb. 04	BB	@ UCLA	(A)
	Sun., Feb. 11	BB	vs. North Carolina	(H)
	Sat., Mar. 03	VT	vs. Michigan	(H)
		BB		
	Fri., Mar. 16	VT	@ Alabama	(A)
	Sun., Mar. 18	FX	@ Texas Woman's	(A)
	Sat., Apr. 07	BB	vs. Denver, Iowa, Iowa State, Kentucky, Minnesota	(A) NCAA Regional, Minneapolis
	Fri., Apr. 20	UB	vs. California, Florida, Kentucky, Utah, Washington	(A) NCAA Championship Semifinals II
2019	Sat., Jan. 05	VT	@ Arkansas	(A)
	Sat., Apr. 06	UB	vs. California, Georgia, Kentucky	(A) NCAA Regional, Athens, Round 3
2020	Fri., Jan. 17	VT	@ Alabama	(A)
	Mon., Jan. 20	VT	vs. Arkansas	(H)
	Fri., Feb. 14	VT	vs. West Virginia, TWU	(H)
		UB		
	Fri., Mar. 06	VT	vs. Michigan	(H)

GLOSSARY OF GYMNASTICS TERMS

1/1 turn: A 360-degree turn.

AAU: Amateur Athletic Union.

Acro series: A combination of tumbling skills performed on floor or beam.

Aerial acro: A maneuver in which the gymnast does a full rotation in the air without her hands touching the floor or the apparatus.

All-around: When a gymnast competes and is scored on all four apparatuses (vault, bars, beam, floor) in a single meet either individually or as part of a team competition.

Amanar: A skill on vault named after Simona Amânar of Romania, the first gymnast to perform it at an official Fédération Internationale de Gymnastique (FIG) competition. It involves a round-off onto the springboard and a back handspring onto the vaulting platform, followed by two and a half twists in a back layout salto off the table.

Arabesque: A pose in which the gymnast stands on one leg with her other leg extended behind her, parallel to the floor.

Back extension roll: A skill in which the gymnast rolls back, and with arms held straight, pushes into a handstand, then steps down from the handstand into a lunge position.

Backflip: A move that begins with the gymnast taking off from either one or both feet, then jumping backward and landing on her feet.

Back handspring: A move in which the gymnast flips backward, touching her hands on the ground midway through the flip.

Back hip circle: A skill usually performed on bars in which the gymnast rests on the bar in a front support, then casts away, returns to the bar, and travels around it until coming again to a front support.

Backward roll: A roll in which the gymnast's feet lead and the body and head follow.

Back salto: This skill is performed with the gymnast taking off from two feet, flipping forward or backward in the air, hands not touching the ground. This skill can be performed in a tuck, pike, or straight body position.

Back walkover: A move in which the gymnast transitions from a standing position to a back bridge, then into a standing position again.

Barani: A front flip with a half twist.

Block: A thrust of the shoulders to increase the height or distance the gymnast will travel.

Bridge: A position in which the gymnast supports themselves with hands and feet flat on the ground, pushing their shoulders and hips up.

Bridge kickover: A move in which the gymnast begins in the bridge position, kicks her dominant leg off the ground, transitions into a split-leg handstand, and levers out of the handstand into a lunge with her arms extended in the air.

Cartwheel: A maneuver in which the gymnast begins with a lunge; places her hands on the ground at a 90-degree angle; kicks her feet over her head one at a time, landing each foot in the order they took flight; and lands in a lunge facing the opposite direction from which she took off, with her arms up, her front leg slightly bent, and her back leg extended straight behind her.

Cast: When from a front support on bars, the gymnast pushes her hips off the bar in a hollow body position.

Cast handstand: This skill is performed from a front support position to an extended straight body in vertical over the hand support.

Cheng: A maneuver named for Cheng Fei, a two-time Chinese National Floor Exercise Champion, two-time Chinese National Vault medalist, and the Chinese National Balance Beam Champion in the early 2000s. The move involves a round-off entry with a half twist on the table, followed by a somersault with one and a half twists before landing.

Clear hip circle: A backward circling skill in which the gymnast's hips do not touch the bar.

Code of Points: The document that regulates the skill values, special requirements, and scoring of each discipline.

Conditioning: Exercises designed to help a gymnast strengthen her core, leg, and arm muscles so as to improve flexibility and control during the execution of skills and routines.

Connection: Skills that link two or more elements in a routine. Depending upon their complexity and difficulty, they can earn extra tenths in bonus toward the routine's value.

Dismount: The act of getting off an apparatus or the final skill performed in a routine.

Double back: A tumbling skill in which the gymnast completes two consecutive backward saltos in the tuck position.

Double double: A double salto backward with two twists.

Double pike: A double salto in the pike position.

Double-twist: Two twists in a straight body position.

Eagle grip: When a gymnast puts her arms up with her palms facing forward, then turns her hands outward 180 degrees.

Elite: The highest level of competition in gymnastics.

FIG: Fédération Internationale Gymnastique, the international governing body of gymnastics.

Flic-flac: Another name for a back handspring.

Flyaway: A dismount from bars in which the gymnast swings and flips off.

Front support: A static hold in which the gymnast compresses her arm muscles, locking them in to support her body before beginning the desired skill.

Front tuck: A move in which the gymnast maintains a tucked position during a front flip.

Front walkover: A move in which the gymnast lifts her legs above her torso into a bridge position and stands up.

Full-in: A maneuver in which the gymnast performs a double salto with a full twist during the first salto.

Full-out: A maneuver in which the gymnast performs a double salto with a full twist during the second salto.

Full-twisting double tuck: A move involving two flips and one full twist.

Full-twisting layout: This move is also known as a **back-full** or **full** and consists of a backward full-twist in the straight body position.

Giant: A skill in which the gymnast rotates 360 degrees around a bar with their body in a fully extended position.

Glide kip: A skill in which the gymnast swings in a piked hollow position, with her toes in front, under the bar, to extend into a straight hollow position parallel to the floor, then pulls them up to the bar along with her hips to arrive in a front support. It may be used as a mount or connecting skill.

Gym Slam: When a gymnast scores a perfect ten on each of the four apparatuses.

Handspring: A connecting maneuver in which the gymnast takes off on both feet and jumps forward placing her weight on her arms so she can push off her hands either forward or backward before landing on her feet.

Handstand: A skill in which the gymnast stands in an inverted vertical position, supporting and balancing her body on her hands.

Hecht: A dismount in which the gymnast releases the apparatus at the height of her backswing, propelling her forward with outstretched arms and legs, and lands upright on her feet.

Heel-snap turn: A turn that occurs on one foot as the gymnast lifts her other foot slightly off the ground, taps her ankle, and holds it there until the move is completed.

Jaeger: A release on the uneven bars in which the gymnast swings backward in an L grip or reverse grip and does a front flip in either a tuck, straddled, piked, or layout position before regrasping the bar.

Jump: When a gymnast takes off from both legs.

L grip: Arms are twisted 360 degrees from under grip, through over grip, thumbs pointing away from the body.

L position: When a gymnast rests her body weight on her hands, leaning her torso slightly forward, and holding her legs horizontally at a right angle to the torso.

Layout: A salto or flip in which the gymnast's body is completely stretched, with her toes pointed and her legs held straight.

LA turn: At body's longitudinal axis turn.

Long hang kip: A kip performed on the high bar.

Long hang pullover: A pullover performed on the high bar.

Lunge: A position in which one leg is flexed approximately 90 degrees in the front and the other leg is straight and extended in the back. The body is stretched and upright over the flexed leg.

Mount: The skill a gymnast uses to get on an apparatus.

NCAA: National Collegiate Athletic Association, which is a nonprofit organization that regulates student athletics among roughly 1,100 American, Canadian, and Puerto Rican schools.

NGA: National Gymnastics Association.

Needle kick: A maneuver in which the gymnast places two hands and one leg on the floor, then kicks the other leg into a full split.

One touch warm-up: A short warm-up on the apparatus in the arena immediately before competition.

Pak: A common high-to-low transition on bars. This salto begins with the gymnast facing the low bar before casting to a handstand, swinging down, then letting go of the high bar as her feet rise above the low bar.

Passé: A position in which the gymnast bends one leg with her toe pointed and places it against the inside of the knee of the supporting leg.

Pike: A position in which the gymnast's body is bent only at the hips, forming an L shape.

Pirouette: A long axis turn performed inverted with support on the hands.

Pivot turn: When a gymnast places one foot in front of the other and turns on the ball of her foot toward her back leg.

Press handstand: A move in which the gymnast starts from a seated position and, by moving her weight forward, pushes into a handstand.

Pullover: A move on bars in which the gymnast starts off with feet on the floor and, using her arm strength, pulls herself up and over the bar.

Punch front: When a gymnast bounces off the floor from two feet, vault board, or beam rather than taking off from one foot.

Release: When a gymnast leaves the bar to execute a move before grasping it again.

Relevé: The position a gymnast assumes when standing on her toes with her feet extended.

Ring leap: A move on the floor or beam in which the gymnast jumps off with both feet, lifts her legs into a 180-degree or wider split while holding her head back, arching her back, and bending her back leg up as if trying to touch her head.

Round-off: A move similar to a cartwheel, but where the gymnast pushes off the ground, bringing her legs together, landing on two feet facing in the same direction she began in. It is often the lead-in to a tumble.

Salto: A flip where the gymnast rotates around the axis of her hips without hand support.

Shaposh: A low-to-high transition on the uneven bars, named for the Soviet gymnast Natalia Shaposhnikova.

Shaposh half: A low-to-high bar release with a half twist in flight.

Overshoot: The skill that gets the gymnast from the high bar to the low bar on the uneven bars. Also known as a **bail**.

Sissonne: A jump forward from a two-foot takeoff to landing on the forward leg in an arabesque.

Sole-circle dismount: A move in which the gymnast rests her toe on the bar before circling around to dismount.

Split jump: A jump executed with the gymnast's legs separated horizontally by 180 degrees as they would be in a front leg split.

Split leap: A move in which the gymnast begins the leap with one leg in front, switches legs quickly in midair to assume a split position of 180 degrees, and lands with her other leg in front of her.

Squat-on: A move in which, from a cast, the gymnast brings her feet in to squat on the lower bar so she is poised to jump to the upper bar on the uneven bars.

Stalder: When a gymnast performs a 360-degree rotation on uneven bars with the legs in a straddle position by the shoulders and head.

Stepout: When a gymnast lands on one foot, then the other, versus when they land on both feet at the same time.

Straddle jump: A jump in which one of the gymnast's legs is held straight out to the left and the other is held straight out to the right at 180 degrees.

Stretch jump: A move in which the gymnast jumps, keeping her body fully extended, toes pointed, and arms stretched high.

Stuck landing: A perfect landing executed without any missteps, stumbles, or errors.

Switch leg leap: A leap forward of at least a 120-degree split with a change of legs to a 180-degree split.

Switch ring leap: A move that involves switching legs midleap while arching the back and throwing the head back, and a 90-degree bent back leg.

Tap swing: A swing on bars that uses the gymnast's change in body position to generate the speed and power necessary for release moves and dismounts.

Tkatchev: A move named after Aleksandr Tkachyov. It is a skill on the uneven bars where the gymnast swings backward traveling over the bar in a straddle position before regrasping it on the other side.

Toe hand: When a gymnast places her toes on the bar, either one foot first or both feet at the same time, to keep her hips from touching the bar. When she is upside down, she then removes her feet from the bar and shoots up into a handstand.

Toe-on full: A toe-on circle into a 360-degree pirouette.

Toe-on half: A toe-on circle into a 180-degree pirouette.

Tsuk (Tsukahara): A vault/family of vaults named after Mitsuo Tsukahara—a five-time Olympic gold medalist. The vault began as a half turn off the springboard onto the vault table, then a push backward, usually into a back salto layout. It has now come to mean any vault that has a handspring with a 1/4–1/2 turn onto the vault table into a salto backward.

Tuck: A jump in which the gymnast bends her knees to her chest.

Twist: A layout with axial body rotation in addition to the rotation turning to the right or the left.

Underswing dismount: A release move from the high bar or the low bar on the uneven bars.

USA Gymnastics: The national governing body for gymnastics in the United States, responsible for selecting and training national teams for the Olympic Games and World Championships.

USAIGC: United States Association of Independent Gymnastics Clubs.

Value Parts: Each level has a set number of value parts required per event.

Yamashita: A vault named after Haruhiro Yamashita, a Japanese gymnast who won two gold medals in the 1964 Summer Olympics. This vault is very close to a handspring in execution.

Yurchenko: A vault/family of vaults named after Natalia Yurchenko, a Soviet gymnast who won the Women's All-Around gold medal in the 1983 World Championships. It begins as a round-off onto the springboard and a back handspring onto the vaulting table, followed by a salto, and is now considered any vault with a round-off–back handspring entry.

Yurchenko double pike: A round-off onto the springboard followed by a back handspring onto the vault, followed by two backflips in the pike position.

ACKNOWLEDGMENTS

Writing a book can be a lot like preseason training. It was intense at times. But much like my experience in the gym, I had a lot of people coaching and cheering me along as I wrote.

My parents, John and Gina Nichols, are by far my greatest life coaches. I couldn't have lived my story, let alone told it here, if it weren't for their consistent love, support, and guidance. My brothers Steve, Sam, and Danny have always been a part of my team as well. I am grateful to them for being great role models and for always encouraging me to be my best. I am also fortunate to have grandparents, aunts, uncles, and cousins who have encouraged my dreams. A special shout-out goes to my Aunt Theresa. While many of my loved ones helped me get to where I am today, she actually drove me to practice far too many times to count!

I also wish to thank Trent Brown for his continuous support, not only as I worked on this book, but as I pursue all my goals and dreams.

Warmest thanks to all my wonderful teammates at TCT; my best friend since childhood, Ally Blixt; my closest friends during my elite years, especially my best friend at the time, Simone Biles; my dearest friend throughout college and beyond, Bre Showers; each and every one of my teammates at OU who were at my side through it all creating amazing memories together; and the gymnastics fans who supported me for so long. I wouldn't be where I am today without you all!

As many of you may have noticed, parts of this book read like an homage to my gymnastics coaches, Mike Hunger, Sarah Jantzi, Rich Stenger, Sami Wozney, K. J. Kindler, Lou Ball, and Tom Haley; my trainer, Jenn

Richardson; and my volunteer coach, Ashley Kerr. That is for a good reason: They each cared deeply about me as a person, not just as a competitive gymnast, which contributed immensely to my personal growth. I am grateful to them all. Extra thanks go to Mike, Sarah, K. J., and Jenn for recounting some of their memories as I was writing this book. Many of their recollections made me smile, jogged a few of my own memories, and reminded me of important details to include.

Dr. Robert Anderson and Dr. James Gannon, of the Summit Orthopedics surgery group, are not only two of the doctors who helped piece me together when I was injured, they also took the time to help me piece together my treatment and surgical history for this book. I am especially grateful to them for providing all the right medical terminology! Special thanks also go to my doctors at the University of Oklahoma, Dr. Matt Dumigan, Dr. Theodore Boehm, and Dr. Stuart Holden.

Competition judge Melissa Ruffino fact-checked a lot of the gymnastics information provided throughout the book. I am so glad I had an expert spotting me so I didn't falter when defining certain skills or discussing the complexities of event scoring. Many thanks, Melissa.

One of my heroes, as you know by now, is attorney John Manly. I wish to express my heartfelt thanks to him for representing survivors of sexual assault every day. I am also very grateful for his help on this book. His input and his review of the legal details was vital.

I must also thank my agent, Sheryl Shade of Shade Global, for setting me off on this journey. You always point me in the right direction of opportunity and new adventure!

To my collaborator, Hope Innelli, for her continuous guidance throughout this amazing journey. I wouldn't have been able to do it without her.

The whole team at Roaring Brook Press, Macmillan Publishing Group, has also been phenomenal. Many thanks to Senior Vice President and Publishing Director Allison Verost and of course much gratitude to Executive Editor Emily Feinberg, whose perspective and input was invaluable from the first draft to the last. Additional thanks to Emilia Sowersby, Abby Granata, Sarah Gompper, Jackie Dever, Joshua Rubins, and Alice Park.

    I certainly hope I didn't miss anyone, but if I did, please know that my heart is full of thanks to *everyone* who helped make this book possible.

    And finally, warm thanks to all of you for buying this book, and reading it to these last pages!